"A must-read for pedagogy... Gannon's explorations into his... the students and the environment... front and center for the rest of us to consider. This work isn't about reform, but transformation, and Gannon's book pushes us in the right direction."

—José Luis Vilson, author of *This Is Not a Test: A New Narrative on Race, Class, and Education*

"In a time of precariously employed professors, crushing student debt burdens, and cynically manufactured campus outrages, *Radical Hope* is a much-needed practical and principled reminder of the promise and possibility of education for liberation."

—Nikhil Pal Singh, author of *Race and America's Long War* and faculty director, NYU Prison Education Program

"This is the book I needed to read—it was a fresh drink of water in a time of turmoil and despair in education. Gannon grounds his calls for radical hope in the work of educational scholars like Freire, hooks, and Giroux, and offers helpful examples and recommendations based on his years of teaching experience. He tackles real issues we are facing at our institutions head-on without capitulating to clichés or trendy solutions often offered in books about higher education."

—Amy Collier, Middlebury College

TEACHING AND LEARNING IN HIGHER EDUCATION
James M. Lang, Series Editor

Other titles in the series:

RADICAL HOPE

a teaching manifesto

kevin m. gannon

West Virginia University Press
Morgantown

ISBN
Cloth 978-1-949199-50-5
Paper 978-1-949199-51-2
Ebook 978-1-949199-52-9

Library of Congress Control Number: 2019044496

Book and cover design by Than Saffel / WVU Press

To Debbie, for everything.

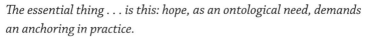

The essential thing . . . is this: hope, as an ontological need, demands an anchoring in practice.

—Paulo Freire, *Pedagogy of Hope*

CONTENTS

—

ACKNOWLEDGMENTS

—

This manifesto's journey from blog post to book has taken much longer, and was far more circuitous, than I originally anticipated. As it turns out, writing a book about hope posed some . . . challenges in our current historical moment. That you're reading this is testament to the many forms of support I've received from various quarters throughout the writing process.

For the last fifteen years, I've been fortunate to work with so many dedicated colleagues and determined students at Grand View University. Not every institution has a culture that genuinely values teaching and is truly student-centered (my own professional experience has driven that point home), so I appreciate working at one that does. I've learned a great deal from both my fellow faculty and staff members, as well as the hundreds of students I've had in my classes, and those lessons suffuse this entire book. My colleague and longtime learning-community collaborator Amy Getty has been a profound influence on my work with students. I've benefited greatly from the wise and empathetic mentorship of Pam Christoffers, the founding director of our teaching center and current associate vice president for institutional effectiveness. I am grateful for the support that my provost,

Carl Moses, has provided for my work and the work of our teaching center throughout his tenure.

A number of friends and colleagues have shaped my ideas about teaching, learning, justice, and inclusion, and this book is better because of them. I'm thankful for the opportunities I've had (either in person or online) to learn from Lee Skallerup Bessette, Val Brown, Sarah Rose Cavanagh, Robin DeRosa, Blake Dye, Peter Felten, Kris Giere, David Gooblar, Paul Hanstedt, Nate Holdren, Caroline Ives, Rajiv Jhangiani, Paul Martin, Doug McKee, Natalie Mendoza, Sean Michael Morris, Raul Pacheco-Vega, David Perry, Ian Petrie, Jerod Quinn, Sherri Spelic, Jesse Stommel, José Vilson, Audrey Watters, and Kevin Yee. I'm particularly grateful to Josh Eyler, Cyndi Kernahan, and Katie Linder for their friendship, perspective, and generous mentoring. Bonni Stachowiak graciously invited me to appear on the *Teaching in Higher Ed* podcast to talk about the original version of my manifesto, and that conversation became the genesis of this book. When I was in the early stages of writing, a couple of wonderful visits with Joanne Freeman provided a much-needed boost; thank you, friend. Online writing sprints with Heather Cox Richardson helped get me out of more than one rut. While writing this book, I drank enough coffee to float a midsized merchant marine convoy; I want to thank the staff at Mars Café in Des Moines for creating what became my best writing space.

I appreciate the opportunities I've had to present some of the ideas in this book, as well as earlier versions of some chapters, at Columbus State University, Elizabethtown College, Gettysburg College, Grinnell College, Iowa Western Tech Community College, MacEwan University, the National Technical Institute for the Deaf at the Rochester Institute of Technology, Oregon State University, Southern Oregon

University, the State University of New York at Fredonia, Sweet Briar College, the University of Colorado at Boulder, the University of Mary Washington, the University of Wisconsin at River Falls, and the University of Wisconsin System's Faculty College. The questions and conversations during these visits were invaluable in helping me articulate and refine my ideas.

Jim Lang has been a friend, mentor, and wise and sage editor. I was honored by his invitation to write for this series, and his supportive and kind feedback made this a much better book. Over a decade ago, I clumsily pitched a half-baked book idea to Derek Krissoff at the annual meeting of the Organization of American Historians. Now, a couple of presses later for Derek and with a completely different project for me, I'm pleased to work with him on this book, which I guarantee is at least three-quarters baked. Amy Collier and another anonymous reviewer provided generous and thoughtful reviews of the final manuscript, and I am tremendously grateful for their insights and affirmation.

Anyone who has pets knows that they are a unique combination of companion, therapist, and entertainment. It is no exaggeration to say that without the particularly zen-like sensibilities of Xena and Megatron the cats and my dogs LuLu and Yoshi, this book wouldn't have been the same. Sometimes one must live in the moment, particularly if that moment involves either playtime or naps.

My children Emma and Leo contributed to this book in ways that might not be quantifiable, but were essential nonetheless. Their good humor, extravagant individuality, and fundamental decency are a constant source of joy and inspiration. They remind me daily of the vital importance of hopeful, caring teaching and learning. I'm grateful for the encouragement and support from my father Mike and stepmother Kelley, and my mother Pat and her partner Steve. My wife, Debbie, lent her perspective as a university administrator to numerous conversations about the ideas in this book, and her keen insights influenced significant portions of the text. Her support, patience, and good humor remind me of what's truly important; I am grateful to have shared this journey with my best friend.

INTRODUCTION

—

It has never been more difficult to teach in higher education than in our current moment. Nearly all of our postsecondary institutions, two- and four-year colleges and universities, are reeling from decades' worth of financial strangulation, the fruit of a neoliberal, market-driven ideology with little room for the notion of a public good. In our classrooms, many of which exhibit the effects of years' worth of deferred maintenance, we have fewer resources with which to teach more students. Most of us, numerically speaking, do this teaching in a precarious position as adjunct and contingent faculty. Even for those of us who are tenured or on the tenure track, those guarantees mean less than they did in earlier periods; tenure is under assault across the country, and funding cuts that eliminate entire programs do not distinguish between tenured and untenured. The academic job market is a smoldering crater; faculty hiring and compensation are well below the levels we actually need to accomplish our missions. Academic freedom is under siege as grandstanding politicians decry "leftist" universities while right-wingers funding institutes at those same universities demand control over hiring and curricular decisions. Moreover, the general public is souring on higher education. A college education was once the epitome of the American dream; now, a majority of one political party believes colleges and universities have "a negative effect" on the United States, while others despair about the increasingly devastating financial burdens of higher education.[1] And the nexus of all these trends is the environment in which we, as faculty, are expected to be effective—even transformative—teachers.

It has also never been more difficult to learn in higher education than in our current moment. To be a college student today requires an element of financial risk and economic uncertainty that would have been inconceivable to prior generations. The rise of the "gig economy," the curious economic spectacle of a "jobless recovery," and skyrocketing costs of living mean that the future looks much more uncertain to today's students than it did for their forebears. To even get to that future, current students must shoulder an unprecedented amount of the costs of higher education themselves, as loans have become the primary means of financing the ever-increasing expense of a college education. In this climate of anxious uncertainty, it isn't surprising that a record number of college students struggle with mental health difficulties. What's more, funding cuts to K–12 education have mirrored, and in some areas outpaced, those that have plagued higher education. The result has been a larger number of underserved and underprepared students entering college. They then find themselves lacking some of the basic academic skills necessary for success, and despite the proliferation of developmental courses and academic support services, retention and graduation rates among these at-risk students have remained flat.[2]

Nor have our campus climates served all of our students well. Students of color attending classes in buildings named after eighteenth- and nineteenth-century slaveholders, for example, can testify to the prevalence of racial prejudice and microaggressions on most of our campuses. The alarming data on campus sexual harassment and assault demonstrates that for women, higher education is often not a safe space.[3] A recent spike in the number of hate incidents on campuses underscores how even such a basic act as going to college is actually a threat for some of our students, who see more concern from their administrators for the right of neo-Nazis and white supremacists to have a campus platform than for their safety and well-being.[4] For today's students, the road to a college degree is fraught with uncertainty, obstacles, risk, and anxiety. For many of them, higher education is a protracted exercise more akin to siege warfare than a journey of development and discovery.

This is probably not the way you expected a book on "radical hope" to begin. This litany of problems and obstacles both faculty and students face on a daily basis seems designed to instill despair, not hope. Indeed, a weary cynicism is both an eminently understandable and frequent response to these conditions. But jaded detachment, tempting as it may be for no other reason than self-defense, is ultimately a trap—one into which we'll drag students along with us if we fall. We've all encountered the grumpy, cynical faculty colleague who ceaselessly complains about their students, the institution, and likely many of their colleagues as well. *The kids can't write a coherent sentence. They don't study. They're on their phones all class period. The administration doesn't give a damn about us. If we have one more useless department meeting, I swear I'll go insane.* Often, but not always, this colleague's cynicism is born out of decades of frustration as the gulf between their sense of vocation and their perceptions of the institutional environment has become impassable. I don't think any of us start our careers teaching in higher education with this bitter sense of betrayal and impotence. Even if we've been battered by the vicissitudes of graduate education and the academic job market, we still want to enter our classrooms and make a difference for our students. The question becomes, then, how do we avoid ending up in a place where we don't believe that what we do matters, and where we surrender to cynical detachment?

I propose that we answer cynicism with purpose, despair with hope. "Hope" is a pretty elastic term, though, and it often becomes a hollow platitude that substitutes itself for the actual work of change. *I have hope in the future*, the thinking goes, *so I just need to survive the present; this too shall pass.* But hope without action is merely fantasy. For those of us committed to changing higher education for the better, to making a genuine difference in our classrooms and on our campuses, a commitment to *radical hope* offers the chance to do so in a clear-eyed and sustainable manner without succumbing to hostile resignation or burned-out despair. As Jonathan Lear puts it, "what makes . . . hope radical is that it is directed toward a future goodness that transcends the current ability to understand what it is. Radical hope anticipates a good for which those who have the hope as yet lack the appropriate concepts with which to understand it."[5] To operate from a place of radical hope, though, is a daunting prospect. It requires us to discern ways of being and acting that are far from clear, and to articulate goals that only exist "at the horizons of one's understanding."[6] Hope, as Rebecca Solnit has famously declared, "is not a lottery ticket you can sit on the sofa and clutch, feeling lucky. It is the axe you break down doors with in an emergency."[7] Radical hope eschews despair, but does so in a way that often relies upon the faith that our current thinking and actions will create a better future—even without specifically understanding what that future will look like.

Teaching is a radical act of hope. It is an assertion of faith in a better future in an increasingly uncertain and fraught present. It is a commitment to that future even if we can't clearly discern its shape. It is a continuing pedagogical practice rather than a set of static characteristics. Simply put, we teach because we believe it matters. That may be hard to remember when we're driving dozens of miles from one adjunct gig to another, or when we're buried beneath a pile of papers to grade, or when we get the dean's email about further cuts to our department's operating budget. Yet that's when it's most evident, if we really think about it. Our most quotidian practices—even and especially in environments of adversity—are a constant assertion that through our work with and among our students we are creating a better future. The very acts of trying to teach well, of adopting a critically reflective practice to improve our teaching and our students' learning, are *radical*, in that word's literal sense: they are endeavors aimed at fundamental, root-level transformation. And they are acts of *hope* because they imagine that process of transformation as one in which a better future takes shape out of our students' critical refusal to abide the limitations of the present.

What does it look like to teach with radical hope, then? "Imagining a process of transformation" sounds nice, but how do we do that when we're tasked with teaching a 500-student lecture section of Psychology 101? I think it is essential for our pedagogy to remain centered in a clear set of principles that we not only put into practice, but make explicit to our students as we invite them to share in our vision. That's an ethic we can apply in a small seminar room or large lecture hall, in an introductory general-education course or an advanced practicum, in a two-year or four-year college, in a public or private university. If hope without action is fantasy, then principles without practice are useless. Hope is the combination of aspiration and agency. Paulo Freire, the Brazilian educator and intellectual godfather of what's become known as critical pedagogy, insisted on the primacy of "praxis." Praxis, in Freirean terms, is the blend of "*reflection* and *action* aimed at the structures to be transformed."[8] Reflection without action has no power, while action without reflection cedes its meaning. A pedagogical praxis centered in radical hope is one that fosters openness and inclusivity, critical reflection, dialogue and conversation, and a commitment to making higher education accessible and meaningful for *all* of our students.

In the pages that follow, I set out my manifesto for teaching and learning, a manifesto staking claim to a better future even within our specific present. Ever mindful of Freire's injunction to combine reflection and action, I ground this manifesto in distinct theoretical terrain but also focus on specific ways in which we can translate that theory into our actual teaching practices. The following chapters function similarly to a set of concentric circles, centered in our individual philosophies, approaches, attitudes, and practices but radiating outwards into the larger settings of classrooms and institutions as a whole. At the end of each chapter, to foreground the importance of praxis, I offer a few points for discernment and reflection as the first steps in putting principles "into practice" (the title for these sections).

Radical hope needs to be more than a slogan; it has to be the set of lenses through which we see our pedagogy, our students, and our institutions. This book is meant to help with that discernment. What I offer here is not *the* way, but *one* way in which we can meet the challenges of our present with practices that embody our faith in a better future for us and our students. Most importantly, though, over and throughout this manifesto is the unwavering belief that teaching is a radical act of hope.

Now let's get radical.

CHAPTER 1

CLASSROOMS OF DEATH

The title for this chapter may strike you as a bit over-wrought, if not downright bizarre. But its origins are less sinister than they seem. I'm drawing upon the imagery of a nineteenth-century philosopher and theologian who, as it turned out, had a good deal to say about education as well. The university at which I currently teach was founded as a "folk school" by Danish immigrants in 1896. When I joined the faculty, I noticed a few nods to this tradition: we fly the Danish flag next to that of the United States in front of our administration building, for example, as befits the sole remaining Danish Lutheran college in the United States (admittedly, never a large group to begin with). But as I learned more about the college's history, I began to discern some particularly interesting aspects of this institutional identity. For example, while "lifelong learning" seems to be quite the vogueish phrase across higher education, my university has embedded the phrase in lots of places, endowing it with more significance than would inhere in just an admissions brochure or marketing buzzword. As it turns out, lifelong

learning was a central tenet of the Danish folk school movement that emerged in the nineteenth century, due primarily
to the writings and influence of Nikolai Frederik Severin
(N. F. S.) Grundtvig. Grundtvig was one of Denmark's most
renowned polymaths and philosophers and was also a principal architect of a resurgent nationalism during the so-called
Danish Golden Age of the mid-1800s. A significant portion
of his writings address education, ranging from critiques
of the current guiding philosophies of higher education to
advocating for specific pedagogies.

What struck me most as I was skimming through some
of this work was a scathing critique of the educational orthodoxy of his day. As a general rule, I am here all day for
revolutionary hot takes on the educational status quo, so I
was immediately intrigued by what I was reading. Grundtvig
had little patience for what he saw as the deadening and
soulless landscape of European (in particular, German and
Scandinavian) higher education. A curriculum centered on
areas like classical languages and rhetoric was elitist, he
believed, and of no relevance or use in the regular lives of
most citizens. What was needed instead, Grundtvig argued,
was a "school for life." This type of institution would provide
education in areas that would not only edify learners, but
prepare them to be good citizens who contributed to the
cultural growth and prosperity of Denmark. It would also
vastly expand the number of learners, removing schooling
from its cloister among the wealthy and powerful and plac-
ing it squarely in the public sphere. Moreover an emphasis
on learning as a lifelong pursuit would ensure continuing
cultural vitality among the populace. To underscore the utility and relevance of his schools for life, Grundtvig castigated
the extant practice of higher education as hopelessly bound
up in stultifying tradition. Rather than institutions that

contributed to the "life" of the country, Grundtvig—never one to skimp on the rhetorical firepower—dubbed them "schools of death." This distinction was at the heart of the folk school movement that became a significant part of the Danish educational landscape. Folk schools (primarily at the secondary level, though Grundtvig also called for the creation of a People's University) embraced Grundtvigian ideas on curriculum and pedagogy, emphasized subjects with practical application (that is, those that enabled full participation in cultural and civic life), and embodied what today we would call a mind-body-spirit approach to teaching and learning. What is noteworthy about this model (which Grundtvig was advocating as early as 1838) is its emphasis on *access*.[1] Grundtvig didn't frame it in those terms himself, but his call for an education that spoke directly to the lives and needs of ordinary citizens, a call that eschewed the then-current model of higher education as irredeemably elitist and therefore alienating for most potential students, resonates quite profoundly with the present-day calls for improving access and inclusion in our institutions of higher education.

Critiques + Possibilities = Hope

The Grundtvig-inspired folk school movement continues today, though it seems to be more prominent in Europe than in North America.[2] But Grundtvig's irascible and blunt dismissal of ossified institutions failing to serve the needs of all the people in their ambit resonates far more widely. Indeed, while they would likely define ideal curricula and pedagogies much differently, critical pedagogues like Paulo Freire and bell hooks echo Grundtvig's call for a life-affirming (as opposed to soul-killing) education. hooks, for example, famously calls for education to be "the practice of freedom," while Freire's vision of educating for critical consciousness ("conscientização") also embraces the life-affirming aspects of a truly vital and reciprocal approach to teaching and learning.[3] This melding of what Henry Giroux called the "language of critique" and the "language of possibility" is an essential part of any pedagogy that claims to be centered in hope.[4] It's all too easy for us to burn ourselves up with nonstop critique to the point where we're merely fighting for the sake of fighting, and have turned ourselves into pedagogical nihilists. But it's just as easy to blithely float along on empty platitudes, lulled like modern-day lotus eaters sustained by inspirational quotes we find on Pinterest telling us dreams can come true in the classroom. It's vital for us to effectively strike the balance between the two; we must be relentless critics of the current neoliberal fetish for schools of death, but we must always do so in the service of a larger vision of what instead could be, as Grundtvig attempted to do with his call for schools of life. It's easy to critique, but harder to build. Yet we owe it to ourselves and our students not only to point out the vast array of problematic areas of the higher educational landscape but also to offer tangible and meaningful alternatives. Neither the language of critique nor the language of possibility is powerful enough on its own; only working in tandem can they help us create a pedagogy grounded in radical hope.

How, then, do we maintain this all-important balance? How do we offer a sustained and vigorous critique of our present that is also grounded in a specific and meaningful program for an achievable future? An important place to begin answering these questions is in a consideration of the ultimate ends of higher education. What is the point of this venture? What is the purpose of higher education? To be sure, we're thinking about these things a lot at the institutional level—or at least we say we are. If your campus is anything like mine, we wrangle about our purpose all the time: we wonder if our core curriculum reflects the aspirations we have for a "truly educated" citizen, and we talk to prospective students and their families about the lasting value of a degree, for example. We resort to claims about "agile graduates" and the marketability of our credentials when we feel compelled to defend our value to external constituencies. But these conversations don't often dip too far below the surface; they basically amount to "education is important because education is good." That's not wrong, but it's also not enough. What are our students actually *doing* (in more than merely the skills-based sense) with what they've received in their higher educational journeys? And does it align with what we think ought to be the purpose of higher education?

The Ends We Seek

In August 2017, the "Unite the Right" rally in Charlottesville, Virginia, saw a range of white supremacist, alt-right, and neo-Nazi groups converge on the town, ostensibly to protest the removal of Confederate monuments. The rally's true purpose, however, was racist fearmongering and violence. The night before the rally, a throng of white men carrying tiki torches and shouting such slogans as "Jews will not replace us" wound its way through the University of Virginia's grounds. The rally itself was marked by dozens of attacks instigated by the alt-right and white nationalist groups, including the severe beating of an African American man in a nearby parking garage as well as the death of one counterprotester (and injury of several more) when a white supremacist sped his car through a crowd of antiracist demonstrators. One of the most emblematic images from this orgy of hate and violence was a close-up photograph of a rank of the tiki-torch marchers, in the center of which walked a young man wearing a polo shirt with the logo of the white nationalist group "Identity Europa," face contorted in anger while screaming whatever slogan the marchers happened to be proclaiming at that moment. Social media users quickly identified him as a current student at the University of Nevada–Reno. Within days, other college students at the rally were identified on social media, including the president of Washington State University's College Republicans. In the immediate aftermath of Charlottesville, these institutions struggled mightily with both the backlash against these students and fallout within their campus communities.[5] Lost in the immediate hubbub over whether those students would be allowed to graduate or if they could even be safely enrolled in classes with students of color, however, was any reckoning with the fundamental question at issue here: *are these the ends we seek in higher education*? To put it bluntly, is it possible for a learner to both successfully move through the academic and intellectual spaces of a college or university and march in support of violent white nationalism?

And if it's possible, *should* it be?

With that question in mind, let's once again ask: What are the ends of higher education, currently constituted? There is a wellspring of tradition from which we (speaking generally) draw when we describe the virtues—indeed, the necessity—of higher education. Sometimes we say it's an agent of social mobility; the nineteenth-century politician and advocate for public education Horace Mann famously declared that "education, then, beyond all other devices of human origin, is the great equalizer of the conditions of men—the balance-wheel of the social machinery," and we've since evoked that sentiment countless times.[6] Sometimes we cite statistics contrasting the average salary over the entirety of one's career between high school graduates and holders of a bachelor's degree. If the boldly mercenary nature of such arguments makes us uncomfortable, we retreat onto loftier grounds. Higher education, we claim, produces new knowledge—it fosters innovation and progress. Yet that argument often returns us to the economic realm, as we tend to couch those things as necessary for "the twenty-first-century economy and workforce," for example. And then we're back into a frame of reference that sees higher education as primarily a skills-training venture, where we produce cogs in the machine, but those cogs have more polish. While the marketability angle may appeal to students and families (rightly) concerned about their future economic prospects, it's not often the place where faculty want to plant our flag. So we fall back onto the "common good" argument: higher education is an engine of democracy, that there is a clear connection between higher education and our larger society, and that higher education thus produces important "civic outcomes."[7] Again, none of this is necessarily wrong. But neither is it enough.

We don't often explore, for example, exactly what the connection between higher education and civil society really *is*. Is it a positive, beneficial connection? Or is it a connection that works to the detriment of one or both parties? How desirable is fostering "innovation" when what's being innovated is a new missile guidance system or the outlines of a labor regime that produces cost efficiencies by degrading the working conditions of human employees? What is the point of creating new knowledge if we are not teaching students (and ourselves) how to use that knowledge or to inquire into its fundamental nature? The college students marching in the ranks of white nationalists at Charlottesville, for instance, believed their education had helped them acquire a lot of new knowledge. One of them, a history major, spoke enthusiastically about the "values" of medieval Europe, which he portrayed as an exclusively "white civilization," when he described how he had become a white nationalist.[8] But that image is not in accordance at all with what the historical evidence, as well as scholarship in medieval studies, tells us. This student may have felt like he had learned "new knowledge," but instead it was no more than a superficial and ultimately illusory claim. This points to the larger dilemma we face: if we couch our aspirations for higher education simply in knowledge creation, we cede any role in the subsequent, and all-important, processes of weighing, analyzing, and acting upon that knowledge claim. Is that what we're about? Knowledge may be power, but power is easily twisted and weaponized. Simply introducing knowledge into the public sphere and then abdicating any role in what happens to it afterwards is at best highly problematic; at worst, it's wildly irresponsible.

This is even more the case when the discussion of higher education conflates, as it so often does, knowledge and skills. When figures identified as thought leaders suggest the real value of higher education rests in its ability to teach new skills to the rising generation (as well as current job seekers who've been left behind, outsourced, or downsized), they cast knowledge and knowledge creation in purely instrumental terms, rendering the work of higher education almost completely transactional in nature. Sure, there are platitudes about "deep learning" and "meaningful connections" thrown into the mix, but that instrumental logic remains the dominant trope. This creates a real problem for those of us engaged in articulating and defending the larger value—the intrinsic public good—of higher education. Challenged by the abstract nature of arguments about social contracts and civic connections, we shift to a language we think will be taken more seriously by administrators, politicians, and cost-conscious parents: the language of marketable skills for the "new economy" and of terms like "nimble" and "agile" and "multiple competencies." But in doing this, we cede the terrain of the debate; we've implicitly declared higher education's real value is transactional and market oriented when we use that language. We've sacrificed our larger vision in favor of short-term relevance. While it might be an eminently understandable move, it's certainly a dangerous one. The "Unite the Right" marchers at Charlottesville were certain in their "knowledge" of how the world works, because they saw no reason not to be. In a larger discourse that treats knowledge as a fixed commodity—a skill set—one has either acquired or lacks, there's no room for questioning.

That's the danger of framing our work and our students' journeys in higher education as discrete processes that have summative, measurable outcomes that are achieved when the student "completes their education." Because what we're really saying is that students have either acquired the necessary knowledge and skills or they haven't, that they have either succeeded or failed, either gotten "what they needed" or failed to do so. Those binaries, in their dismissal of habits like self-examination, critical thinking, and questioning, mistake training for education. The results of such framing are what we see in these fraught times: bigotry and hate wrapped in righteous certitude, the theft of the public sphere, the commodification and marginalization—and thus dehumanization—of ever more people. Classrooms of death (as opposed to learning for life) have helped create a society that's necrotizing before our eyes. And higher education has let that happen in large part because we are afraid to embrace the full implications of how we ought to be talking about the ends we seek. "The events in Charlottesville," Henry Giroux argues, "raise serious questions about the role of higher education in a democracy. What role if not responsibility do universities have in the face of widespread legitimized violence?"[9] Make no mistake: higher education has both a role and a responsibility in creating and sustaining a free, democratic society—whether we admit it or not, whether we're aware of it or not, whether we think it's our job or not, whether we like it or not. If we mean what we say about the intrinsic value and good in our collective enterprise, then we cannot abdicate that role or our responsibility for playing it.

Pedagogy Cannot Be Neutral

The surest way to avoid ceding our place in the process of creating and sustaining a more just, democratic, and free society is not just to do the work, but own the reasons we're doing it. Maybe Grundtvig offers one way to conceive of such a stance in his relentless advocacy for education that seeks vitality (or revitalization) in creating the type of learning spaces we could call "schools of life." These are spaces that see the possibilities that exist beyond and because of our critiques, spaces that invite and include rather than marginalize or exclude, spaces where our students (and us) are seen as people in process rather than a series of benchmarks and competencies. Contrast that vision with its opposite: the "classroom of death," where "knowledge" is simply handed out in discrete chunks and assessed summatively, where students have no agency in the learning process and see their worth decided solely by whether they are deemed proficient in certain skills. The proponents of this life-stealing, joy-killing pedagogy tell us, Paulo Freire warns, "we no longer have any need today of a militant education, one that tears the mask from the face of a lying dominant ideology; that what we need today is a *neutral* education, heart and soul devoted to the *technical training* of the labor force—dedicated to the transmission of content in all the emaciation of its technicity and scientism."[10] Our work is to reject that weary and cynical appeal with a counternarrative of hope, a narrative of teaching and learning practices for a higher educational environment functioning as it *could*, not as it is.

Creating a narrative and embodying it in our practice is an intentional act, a stand on certain foundational principles. To reject classrooms of death and live a pedagogy embracing liberation and hope is deciding to place oneself in particular ethical and political territory. We can't do these things if we see teaching as simply instruction, a mere act of transferring content from our brains to our students' notebooks. We have to approach—and advocate for—teaching and learning as far more than simple content delivery; otherwise, there would be no compelling argument against plopping students down in front of a YouTube playlist for a couple of years and then handing them a degree. This type of open and unabashed advocacy hasn't always fared well in academe, however. Many of us had graduate training in our disciplines that tried to inculcate a reverence for "objectivity," a separation of subject and knowledge that would render our work more "scholarly" and thus "authoritative." Despite the fact that true objectivity is a myth, any challenge to its regime feels transgressive and is likely to be treated as less-than. The regular, everyday work of teaching and research is often predicated on what Laura Rendón has identified as the "agreements" that undergird the dominant practices in higher education. In particular, what Rendón calls "the agreement to privilege intellectual/rational knowing" and "the agreement to avoid self-examination" operate powerfully in much of academia.[11] This peer pressure for neutrality, the unacknowledged disdain for personal introspection as a part of our work, has operated as a cultural imperative to fashion an aura of scholarly detachment. It is so ingrained in higher education in large part due to its reproduction with every cohort of graduate students or disciplinary newcomers. It is a hard tide to swim against.

We see the harmful ways in which this veneration of objectivity plays out in, for example, the ways a predominantly white department characterizes the complaints from its one African American member regarding the lack of attention to diversity in faculty searches as a bothersome playing of the "race card." Or a practitioner in a STEM discipline who responds to data about the lack of women and people of color in the field with the brusque claim that graduate school is designed to produce "the best scientists" no matter what they look like. Or the historian who resists a curriculum reform intended to introduce postcolonial and subaltern studies courses by arguing that "historical significance" should be the sole arbiter of what the department teaches its majors. In these examples, and countless others like them unfolding on campuses across the United States and Canada, the dominant discourse is always the standard for what's objective, and challenges to it are thus framed as deviant, dangerous, and/or unscholarly. This is how we get resistance to inclusive pedagogy that characterizes a decolonized syllabus as mere tokenism, or a denigration of content and "trigger" warnings as pandering to whiny, entitled brats. Much of what I argue constitutes a pedagogy of radical hope, in fact, challenges the general orthodoxy of higher educational institutions and practices. Teaching with radical hope therefore asks us to reject the "agreements" that inform the dominant narrative in favor of asserting our own ethical stance.

I want to be clear, though, that this process will look different depending on who you are and your particular context. It may not be feasible to run the red flag up the pole and vociferously challenge departmental culture if you are a term-to-term adjunct faculty member. Being the only or one of the few women in an overwhelmingly male department brings with it challenges that might prevent an explicit avowal of what could be interpreted as nonscholarly, or "unprofessional," practices. I'm fully aware that challenging dominant narratives brings no small amount of risk, and I believe it's an obligation for those of us with secure platforms and positions to absorb that risk and deflect it from others. However it might look—avowedly public or quietly implicit within one's own practices—that ethical stance is a necessary one for us, though. Neutrality is a luxury of the comfortable; in these uncomfortable times, our students and our academic communities need more from us.

We can no longer hide behind the facade of objectivity. Eschewing political stances is an abdication of our responsibility, and intellectually dishonest to boot. As Henry Giroux has argued:

> The issue is not about whether public or higher education has become contaminated with politics. It is, more importantly, about recognizing that education is already a space of politics, power, and authority. The crucial matter at hand is how to appropriate, invent, direct, and control the multiple layers of power and politics that constitute both the institutional

formation of education and the pedagogies, which are often
outcomes of deliberate struggles to establish particular notions
of knowledge, values, and identity. As committed educators, *we
cannot eliminate politics*, but we can work against a politics of
certainty, a pedagogy of censorship, and institutional forms
that close down rather than open up democratic relations.[12]

It's important to pause here and consider the implications
of Giroux's observations. If the entire landscape of higher
education is political terrain—and I'd argue it most certainly
is—then shying away from being political is to surrender
one's agency within and throughout that entire landscape.
We cannot do this if we believe the work we're doing in community with our colleagues and students is worth sustaining
and expanding. "Political" means so much more than simply
partisan maneuvering or overtly ideological platforms; it
describes any field or space where power relations are contested. Curricula are political, for example; they are assertions of power on behalf of a specific program of knowledge
and skills. Budgets and the allocation of faculty lines are political; they are declarations of where (likely scarce) resources
ought to be allocated, and thus assertions about what truly
matters to the institution. Moreover, the outcomes of these
processes, of curricular revisions or of budget reallocation,
are also statements about what *isn't* important or valued.
(In many institutions, as well as in higher ed writ large, the
humanities tend to occupy that unenviable position.)

A Pedagogy of Radical Hope

Most essentially, *pedagogy is political*. Our pedagogy is a declaration of what we think matters. It's a living description
of how we think good teaching and learning should occur,

and of the moral imperative to create the type of inclusive and equitable learning spaces in which our students become critically conscious and actively engaged in their own education. In avowing this feature of our pedagogy, though, it's essential to remember that statements of theory must be reinforced by concrete practices, or else they'll simply dissipate like any other statement of intent that's never operationalized. Taking a stand on pedagogical principles is a recursive process; we actively choose to take and retake that stand every time we engage with teaching and learning. So what does that process look like? What does it mean in practice to stand for a pedagogy grounded in the ethic of radical hope? What beliefs do we hold to when we embrace the political nature of the pedagogical worldview we choose to embody in our practice? Here are what I see as the most essential features of a pedagogy of hope.

It is life-affirming: I mean this in the dual sense of both fostering lifelong learning and ensuring that teaching and learning are *vital*, as opposed to static and lifeless, processes. To put it in Grundtvigian terms, we mustn't give into the pressures to create classrooms of death. Yet this is precisely what the dominant narratives within higher education have wrought. Indeed, Paulo Freire asserted decades ago that "education is suffering from Narration sickness":

A careful analysis of the teacher-student relationship at any level, inside or outside the school, reveals its fundamentally narrative character. This relationship involves a narrating Subject (the teacher) and patient listening objects (the students). The contents, whether values or empirical dimensions of reality, tend in the process of being narrated to become lifeless and petrified. . . . The teacher talks about reality as if it were motionless, static, compartmentalized, and predictable. Or else he expounds on a topic completely alien to the existential experience of the students. His task is to "fill" the students with the contents of his narration—contents which are detached from reality, disconnected from the totality that engendered them and could give them significance. Words are emptied of their concreteness and become a hollow, alienated, and alienating verbosity.[13]

We cannot shape curricula that are divorced from lived experience. We cannot view knowledge as something to simply be handed out in "lifeless and petrified" chunks, for the recipients to do with as they will. We cannot envisage learning as a process in which content is simply passed from instructor to student in a merely instrumental and transactional fashion. We cannot conceive of students, or allow them to conceive of themselves, as passive spectators. Instead, we should be approaching teaching and learning with a vision of students as dynamic and evolving coparticipants.

It centers student agency: The key to preventing the construction of a passive role for students in higher education is rejecting the narrative that focuses solely on what our students *can't* do. The learning-deficit trope is an insidious attack on the abilities of both us and our students, an insinuation that none of us can change, grow, or develop. But isn't higher education supposed to help students do those very things? If we only see them as what they cannot do when they arrive in our classrooms, then we foreclose on the very process of developing one's potential and prevent students from realizing what should be one of the chief outcomes of higher education. Seeing our students as active partners in teaching and learning, as cocreators of knowledge and coparticipants in the scholarly conversation, affirms and encourages their sense of agency. This, in turn, allows us all to fashion a new narrative, one that emphasizes what Amy Collier and Jen Ross have called "not-yetness."[14] Students can't write? Well, not yet. But they will. Can't do math? Not yet, at least. But our job is to help them find the ways to get closer to yet. Not-yetness urges us to encounter students as people in process, not as fixed and insurmountable deficits. In doing so, we create the spaces in which learning becomes a collaborative—as opposed to performative—process within which our students create and sustain agency.

It is inclusive: None of this work matters if it does not include all of our students. Our learning spaces—however we create and define them, and wherever they exist—must be accessible for all. A pedagogy based on radical hope for our students' futures, as well as the futures they will create, necessarily rests on a foundation of equity. My advocacy of inclusive pedagogy, of paying attention to matters like design, representation, and interaction, throughout this manifesto proceeds from this conviction that all of our students must have an equitable opportunity to participate in their intellectual and academic journeys, and to do so in a learning environment that welcomes, affirms, and supports them.

It is *praxis*: Theory has to be embodied in tangible practice to be meaningful. A pedagogical philosophy must be more than sloganeering; it has to pervade our decisions and actions as well. How do I select readings and other course materials? In what ways can my students and I collaborate in creating the type of environment where meaningful discussions will flourish? How do my assignments intersect with my students' strengths, yet also match the spaces where they need challenging and growth? For teaching and learning to be truly transformative, we need to attend to both reflection *and* action.[15]

A pedagogy standing on these four columns creates an array of possibilities for us and our students. It promotes and suffuses dynamic, open learning spaces. Asserting our belief that the processes of teaching and learning can meaningfully transform the future, that we and our students can be the architects of change, is a proclamation of hope. That proclamation gets its substance from the accumulated effects of our decisions and actions, no matter how quotidian and mundane. It's also the means by which we bring teaching and learning to life for our students and encourage them to become lifelong learners themselves. We can take a stance that affirms vitality, growth, and hope for higher education and our larger society. Indeed, that's far more attractive than persisting in a course that takes away that vitality and creates instead an ossified, lifeless space where learning goes to die.

INTO PRACTICE

Does your institution's curriculum more closely match a "school for life," or does it reflect the "deadening" ethos that someone like Grundtvig would condemn? How about the instructional practices at your institution? Do they reflect whatever the nature of the curriculum is? Reflect on the ways in which your own practice fits—or doesn't fit—into this larger environment, and why that might be the case. Are there places (curricular working groups or committees, perhaps) where you might be able to extend these conversations outward?

What are the "agreements" that create the teaching and learning environment in which you and your students are working? Are they agreements that promote student success, or departmental/institutional stability? Consider a freewrite or journal entry describing the agreements you want to cultivate with your own courses and students.

—

CHAPTER 2

THE THINGS WE TELL OUR STUDENTS

—

Several years ago, I had a student in one of my survey courses who started strong, but began to tail off rapidly by week four or five. She got As on her first quizzes and wrote a really nice essay for the first writing assignment. But then she started missing more classes, and then didn't show up for the mid-term exam. I asked her friend, also in the class, to reach out to her and let her know I needed to speak with her about maybe dropping the course so she wouldn't have an F on her transcript. A few meetings got scheduled, but she broke the appointments and emailed excuses: she was sick, or her car broke down, or an uncle died. I became highly annoyed at what were clearly B.S. stories, and basically wrote off any chance of her passing the class. If she wasn't going to put in the effort, I thought, why should I? She'd get the F, too bad, so sad, so it goes.

A few days later, that student showed up at my office. And she looked awful. She had clearly been sick, looked to have lost weight, and appeared to have not slept for . . . well, quite a while. Voice trembling and tears falling, she told me she'd been afraid to tell me the real reason she'd been missing classes and not doing her coursework; the excuses she'd given me reflected that anxiety, not any attempt to fool me or pull one over. But now, she told me, she wanted to be honest. At this point, I was feeling a mixture of anxiety (What was I about to hear?) and regret (Why had I been so quick to dismiss her stories?), but nothing prepared me for her revelation that she was trying to kick a heroin addiction, and the only available appointment times at the methadone clinic often conflicted with our class meetings. Because of that, and also because her body felt miserable after those treatments, she was falling behind in all her courses. Things were starting to stabilize, though; there was a new treatment schedule and now she wanted to know if there was a way she could make up her missed work and try to get back on track. I don't remember exactly how I responded. But I remember vividly how powerfully I sensed the depth of suffering she'd been experiencing, and how powerfully evident it was that in the midst of *everything*, she remained determined to continue her education. Who was I to close that door, and what would doing so have said to this student—and, by extension, all of my students?

In the end, we were able to come up with an arrangement where she could make up her exam and I would excuse her absences from class as she turned in subsequent assignments. Even though there was another bump or two along the way, she ended up earning a B for the semester (and passed all her other classes as well). I'm still in awe of the effort that victory took. But I remain chastened by this experience, too; if I had persisted in my adversarial stance, I wouldn't have allowed her the chance at that victory. It

makes me sad to think about what the results of that might
have been.

What Do We Say to Our Students?

Not all student struggles are that dramatic, and not every
student is as forthright concerning the source of their struggles. Even in the more mundane cases of struggling students,
though, my approach remains the same. I am their ally, and
learning is our mutual goal. Whatever arrangements can
be the most effective means for getting us to that goal are
the arrangements I want to use. My approach to course and
classroom policy was forged out of both experience and ethics. As I experienced what it really meant to teach on diverse
campuses, I realized the conceptions about things like classroom management that I brought out of grad school and
into my own classrooms were inadequate. There were several
professors from my undergraduate years whom I held up as
models; they were engaging, understanding, compassionate,
and fair. If I wanted to be a similar model for my students, I
concluded, I needed a pedagogy centered on those qualities.
I had to realize that treating all students *equally* was not
the same thing as treating all students *equitably*. Not every
student needs the same amount or types of support; in order
to help all of my students be successful, I would need to be
flexible instead of rigid, adaptable instead of dogmatic.

I had to abandon the vision of myself as a scholar-orator
delivering the knowledge my students would otherwise be
without, and dedicate my teaching to actively involving
students in constructing their own knowledge. With that
commitment came the realization that for each of my students, that process of construction was likely to be distinc-
tively shaped by their own contexts, and I needed to account

for that if I was to effectively assist them in that process. Students were thus not passive recipients of things I had to offer, but rather active partners in a mutual project of higher learning. They weren't an audience, they were my castmates. Allies, not adversaries.

What it really boils down to, I think, is this simple question: *What are we saying to our students?* What do our everyday teaching practices and classroom style say about what we think of them? What messages—whether intentional or not—do we convey to our students? Can they trust us? Are we their allies or adversaries?

What are we saying to our students?

I don't think we ask this question enough, whether it's of our own pedagogy or our institution's practices. When it comes to our courses, though, it's a question that should be front and center as we design and prepare them. Are we telling them that they are creators of knowledge, or merely its passive recipients? Are we telling them we expect them to meet high expectations, or that we think they'll likely try to game the system? Are we saying we value learning, or simply a certain type of performance? Ask yourself: if one of your courses could talk—using everything except your voice—what would it tell your students? What would your syllabus, assignment sheets, textbooks, other readings, and related course materials say about your perception of those students and their abilities? To add a layer to this thought exercise, consider whether every one of your students would be hearing the same message from those materials. Would some students be told one thing while others receive a different, perhaps even contradictory, message? For example, a range of required textbooks authored solely by white men can implicitly suggest to students of color that people like them do not participate in the process of creating knowledge in your field. When we talk about teaching a successful course, most of the time our conversations start with the first day of class. Yet that initial encounter between us and our students unfolds in a learning space that's already been created, whether we're conscious of it or not. What that learning space looks like, how it invites students in or discourages them from entering, can decisively shape our everyday pedagogical practices. To teach so that all our students may learn—to engage in a practice grounded in radical hope for a future shaped by those students—means we have to be aware of what we are really saying to them.

Curricula: Explicit and Hidden

Scholar-practitioners of critical pedagogy have considered this issue—the answer to the question of what we "tell" our students—and discerned a number of unintended outcomes. Conceptualizing this figurative dialogue as "the hidden curriculum," critical pedagogical thought gives us a powerful analytical tool to gain some insight into the ways we talk to our students before ever having the chance to actually utter a word in front of them. The hidden curriculum is best conceived as a sometimes complementary, sometimes contradictory counternarrative to our formal, explicit curriculum (learning objectives, assessments, assignments, and the like). A particular course or program may be structured in a way faculty believe will likely lead to certain outcomes: things like proficiency in research methods or meeting certain field-specific professional standards, for example. But as students move through these learning experiences, there will also be outcomes that are unintended, unplanned for, and sometimes straight-up undesirable; those outcomes are the products of the hidden curriculum. The problem is that learning doesn't just occur as a result of our formal, explicit curricula. The hidden curriculum also embraces what students are learning in our courses and institutions. Sometimes, it's *that* learning that ends up being the most powerful and durable thing students take from our courses and programs.

What does the hidden curriculum actually look like in operation? In what ways are students learning things we had no idea we were even teaching? Think about a particular course at your institution that has the reputation as a "weed-out" class for a particular major. Perhaps the instructor has a first-day tradition of dramatically conveying to students what the class's purpose is. *Turn to your left, now turn to your right*, they intone; *judging by historical averages, one of the three of you will not make it through this semester.* Students who survived this gateway course talk about the demands of upper-level work in the particular program of which it's a part. All-nighters, brutal exams, impossible group projects—there might even be an institutional lore surrounding the program, and an almost perverse pride from some of its members in being the most rigorous or demanding or intense major out there. Now ask what this type of culture is really saying to students. What's really valued here: learning, or endurance? If students major in this program, will they embark on an intellectual journey, or a gauntlet of academic hazing? Are students being told what *really* matters is their readiness to submit to all sorts of draconian requirements inflicted in the name of "rigor," rather than the specific knowledge and habits of mind needed by practitioners of this discipline? Are teaching and learning collaborative projects or performative rituals? Students in the program tend to separate into cliques and view other groups as competition in some sort of zero-sum academic Hunger Games. The faculty might complain that their students keep asking "if this will be on the test," and that students care more about grades than they do learning. But maybe they're just doing as they've been told.

From a particular faculty viewpoint, classes and programs like these might play the role of something like the last bastion of rigor in an increasingly "dumbed-down" academy. The number of students who drop the class or transfer out of the program is a badge of honor. And maybe the content is that hard, or the learning outcomes that important. Maybe it's important to let beginning students know they can expect a difficult road ahead of them. Nothing is inherently wrong with that, but the ways in which those things are communicated to students are rarely neutral. In my experience, programs that embrace this type of culture are also programs that struggle to attract and retain a diversity of students, all while their faculty swear that "you have to be a certain type of student to succeed here." When instructors lament their students only seem to care about what's on the exam, they fail to see that their emphasis on weeding people out has rendered grades existentially important for their students. Students may be learning the type of things articulated in the learning outcomes for that course or program, but they are also learning, for example, that competition trumps collaboration and faculty only respect them when they take up study habits that threaten their health and well-being. They might end up being good engineers, or lawyers, or film critics, but they probably won't be empathetic or thoughtful ones. What they learned through both the formal and the hidden curriculum makes that so.

Perhaps this example seems like a caricature, its worst

traits exaggerated to make a point. Or perhaps it accurately describes something at your particular institution, or maybe even in your own collegiate experience. Examples of the hidden curriculum in action are all around us in academia. When we read studies of gender disparities in certain programs or majors we can discern that what's being said to students in these spaces varies wildly depending on one's gender identity. The "leaky pipeline" in STEM fields, where women and African Americans are dramatically underrepresented, invites us to wonder what's being said (implicitly or explicitly) that welcomes some students into that pipeline, but turns others away. Many of our disciplines are beset by enrollment and retention issues, particularly as they concern women and minoritized students. So we might ask ourselves who we're holding up as the people who create knowledge in our fields; do our students see textbook or monograph authors who look like them? When we complain about our students approaching their coursework in merely transactional terms—*What do I need to do to get a C?*—we should wonder what they're hearing from us that leads to such a fixation upon grade point averages. If students see our class as "an easy A" or if our course's subject matter seems to ratchet up their anxiety levels, there's something they've been told that's prompted these reactions—and thus something we can say to alleviate them. Either way, we need to be intentionally aware of the extent of the hidden curriculum, and the power with which it functions.

Teaching and Learning with Compassion

This type of awareness is vital to creating the type of learning spaces in which all our students can be successful. We may not be able to control all of the narratives surrounding those learning spaces, but we can do a great deal to be conscious of what we're saying to our students—in all senses of the term. In the foreground of that consciousness should be the question, *what do we think about our students?* Our students are most certainly asking that question themselves, and often finding answers in places we didn't intend. Our students cannot succeed in a learning environment in which they think they are devalued or seen as less-than. Learning becomes more difficult when students don't feel like they can trust the instructor. It becomes impossible when students feel like they're being told they don't belong there. I might tell my students I trust them, and they should trust me and feel comfortable enough to come see me if they're encountering any difficulties in the course. But if my syllabus states in bold print that documentation must be provided in order to excuse an absence, even if it's for a funeral or medical visit, then what I'm *really* saying to students is that I don't trust them at all, and that my response to their approaching me with a problem will likely be as callous as demanding a program from the funeral to prove grandma really passed away. When it comes to pedagogy, the old cliché is often true: actions do speak louder than words.

Teaching from a place of radical hope means that we believe every one of our students can succeed in accomplishing what our courses ask of them, and that we commit to acting on that belief. For some of our students, an instructor who actually believes they can not only pass but do well is a novel occurrence, and we shouldn't underestimate the power that being an advocate for our students holds. To be an advocate for student learning, I think we have to be advocates for both students *and* learning. That may seem like an obvious point, but sometimes standard practice in higher education often looks like advocating for one at the expense of the other. For example, when we pound the pulpit in the name of rigor, but put it into practice by simply adding more work and longer projects to an otherwise unchanged course, we are prioritizing an idiosyncratic version of learning, likely at the expense of our students. The same holds true in much of the debate surrounding so-called safe spaces and trigger warnings, where critics of these techniques rail against "snowflakes" in a bizarre performance that does nothing to improve the learning environment. We might think that Facebook and Twitter posts making fun of the number of dead grandmothers in a particular class are a humorous testament to our tough-teacher street cred; funny or not, they certainly don't advocate for our students. So much of our public-facing stance tends to position students as adversaries instead of allies, when it's the opposite that should be true. Our default pedagogical approach should be empathetic and kind. When faced with the choice between compassion and being a hard-ass, it may be less immediately satisfying to choose compassion, but in the long term it's an exponentially more effective means to promote learning.

The need for a fundamental sense of compassion has never been more visible than in our current higher educational context, where institutional resources and morale decline as the diversity and needs of our student population increase. To reverse what's become decades' worth of starvation budgets and an increasingly hostile political-cultural environment for higher education, we need to build a future radically different from our present. The work we do with and among our students—teaching and learning, creating and collaborating, building knowledge and burnishing confidence—is also the work of building that future. But that future can only come to pass if we involve as many students as possible in its creation. A future that's shaped by processes that push significant numbers of students to the margins is one that will end up depressingly similar to our present. To militate against this outcome, we ought to begin dismantling the systems that marginalize our students. That's a practice that starts in our own classrooms, in the routine choices we make every day about how we engage with our students and their stories—about what we say to them. An approach that embraces empathy and compassion as its default orientation is foundational to a pedagogy of radical hope.

INTO PRACTICE

What would students say is the "hidden curriculum" in your department, program, or institution? Consider advocating for a campus climate survey or conducting student focus groups around teaching and learning, if your institution doesn't already do so, to gather data on this issue. You might also use informal and anonymous feedback techniques to survey your own courses.

In your immediate teaching environment, what are the connotations and practices associated with concepts like *rigor* and *compassion*? Is there a culture of one or the other? What implications might that have for your own practices? Consider journaling about your sense of the environment and its effects on the teaching and learning around you.

CHAPTER 3

CULTIVATING TRANSFORMATIVE TEACHING

I talk really, really fast when I get nervous or excited. I know this about myself now, and am able to make allowances for the habit when I feel my speech beginning to accelerate. But I didn't always have this self-awareness, and I struggled in my graduate work and early teaching career to rein in oratory that sometimes ventured into warp-drive territory, especially on occasions where I was in front of an audience. The first time I delivered a paper at a scholarly conference, for example, I blazed through fourteen pages in just over fifteen minutes. It felt like a half hour to me, but I realized how off my assessment was when I looked up at the end and saw the stunned faces of the (admittedly small) audience. The first time I taught a course as the instructor of record, while I was still a PhD student, I fell victim to the same malady, enhanced by my near-maniacal insistence on covering *everything*. For an entire semester, I bombarded a roomful of students with rapid-fire lectures stuffed to the gills with information and detail.

My end-of-semester evaluations were littered with comments along the lines of "oh my God he talks so fast!" and "take a breath, dude!" If any University of South Carolina alumni who sat through my first attempt at teaching the US history survey are reading this: I'm really, really sorry.

I cringe when I remember that semester, even if I've gotten a little better at this teaching thing since then. In retrospect, I had to learn some hard lessons about what I was doing and why I was doing it. As a graduate student, I was moving in an intellectual milieu that placed a premium on things like breadth of knowledge and claims to expertise. I approached my class as if establishing my legitimacy as an expert was more important than establishing rapport, in much the same way that many academics approach Q&A sessions or purportedly social events at conferences. I also placed a premium on coverage, which ended up coming at the expense of meaningful learning. The common denominator here was that my assumptions about how college-level teaching should be conducted implicitly centered on the instructor, not the students. That's not to say that I didn't have good pedagogical role models from my undergraduate work or my master's program; I was lucky enough to have more than a few, actually. But having been so immersed in the scholarly literature and other materials of my discipline over the previous several years, I brought the conference-talk mindset to the survey-course classroom, with predictably suboptimal results. In that mindset, my teaching was performative rather than collaborative, and my students didn't have to look very far for reasons to disengage. Sure, we "covered" everything, but all that meant was I walked around in front of my students and talked (often rapidly) about US history from the beginnings of European colonization through Reconstruction. But data such as student ratings of my instruction and the overall course grade distribution showed learning occurred unevenly, at best.

Who Are We Teaching For?

After this underwhelming experience, it became clear to me that I needed to reassess the assumptions I'd brought with me into the semester. The things that attracted me to the discipline of history—the chance to engage actively with the past, to delve deeply into historical sources, and the rich discussions with like-minded collaborators—were not the things I had offered to my students. In my teaching, I had centered myself and my quest to establish expertise, which meant I was pushing my students and their motivation to learn to the margins. This wasn't what I had set out to do at all! Regardless of intent, it was clear my teaching goals and my actual practice were fundamentally out of alignment. What could explain this disjointedness? I come from a family of teachers, I was passionate about pedagogy even as a graduate student, and I knew teaching was where I wanted to go with this whole academia thing. But my first solo experience had been a mess. I was operating under a flawed assumption of how people learn in teaching as if simple auditory exposure to material meant that a student learned it. Yet that wasn't how I had acquired my own passion for the discipline. Why should I expect my students to connect with history like I had done, if I wasn't building into my courses the things that had inspired me as a student?

Operating from an instructor-centric position like this also leads to a deficit approach when interacting with students. If I'm foregrounding my own expertise as the class benchmark, then my students (who are not professional historians) will always be less-than. It's all too easy to critique novices for not being experts, even though when put in those stark terms, it's an absurd proposition. During my first semester teaching, I actually saw the fruits of this deficit mindset most vividly in the graduate student lounge. There were a handful of us PhD students teaching our own survey courses, and one of my colleagues was endlessly frustrated by what his students couldn't do. *They can't write a thesis! They don't know any history! They don't read! They can't carry on a discussion!* That was the litany: the students were never going to amount to anything; this was the worst class ever; if this is the future, we're screwed. For the rest of us, this got old real fast. It's one thing to vent about students—that's a long-standing educator tradition. It's another thing entirely to declare that your entire class was a collection of hopeless stumps. I mean, is it really possible that all seventy-five or so students in this class had literally never written a paper or read a book? The law of averages alone suggests that my colleague's jaundiced view was inaccurate. Yet as I rolled my eyes when I heard for the thousandth time how historically illiterate today's students were, I had the realization that my own implicit view of student learning wasn't too far from his. If I taught by straight, rapid-fire lecture in order to cover the material, then I was essentially telling my students I didn't think they could learn anything on their own, or with one another. Rather, my actions were a declaration that learning would be an essentially passive endeavor for them, that knowledge wasn't something they could create but rather some arcane commodity they could only receive through my mediation. Maybe I wasn't holding court in the grad lounge and yelling about what students couldn't do; but if I was honest with myself, I could see that my pedagogy operated under the same basic assumptions.

That was the moment it clicked for me: if I didn't want to

be That Guy—the one already jaded and cynical before his teaching career even really started—then it wasn't enough to simply avoid talking like him. I had to stop teaching like That Guy, too. I needed to reflect on what I really wanted my pedagogy to be about: would teaching be a way for me to perform my expertise, or would it be about connecting students with what I knew history could do for their own intellectual growth and agency? In short, I needed to step out of the center and allow my students to be there instead. To be charitable, this isn't something that someone teaching their first class is necessarily going to realize; rookie mistakes and the opportunity to grow from them are an essential part of anyone's pedagogical process. But I've learned that this process unfolds best through embracing a pedagogy that puts students and their learning at the center.

When we adopt a student-centered philosophy, the possibilities for a truly transformative pedagogy open before us. But that transformative power must be intentionally cultivated; it doesn't merely *poof* into existence as the result of mouthing a few platitudes about active learning techniques. Truly transformative pedagogy is *radical*, in the literal sense of the term: it asks us to engage in root-level, fundamental changes to not only our own designing and teaching, but our institutional structures and cultures as well. If we aim to teach from a place of radical hope instead of jaded cynicism, then we have to challenge many of the "agreements" (to once again use Laura Rendón's term) shaping the milieu of higher education. These agreements represent the so-called givens, the common-sense reality of higher education; simply put, they are what we (speaking of higher education as a whole) have "agreed" to be the hegemonic consensus that guides the behavior of us and our institutions. We have, for example, agreed to have hierarchical relationships—professor and student, expert and novice—serve as the default dynamic within higher education (Rendón calls this "the agreement of competition"). As I discussed in chapter 1, we've agreed "to privilege intellectual/rational knowing," that a Western-style, Enlightenment-influenced epistemology is the coin of the realm. We agree that student and material—the learners and the learned—are separate entities ("the agreement of separation"), and the goal of education is to fill the former with the latter until we reach capacity.[1] These agreements are part of the water in which we all swim, and like the fish in David Foster Wallace's story, we generally don't even realize we're in the water to begin with.[2] Rendón's use of the word "agreement" is important, in that it illustrates how many aspects of the higher educational environment are not simply faits accompli, but rather the product of actual choices by actual people. This is a crucial point, because it empowers us to declare that if those agreements are unsatisfactory, then we should choose something else.

Pedagogical Bankruptcy

The type of interactions that traditional academic culture mandates between teachers and students is one of those unsatisfactory agreements. Even if we don't tend to see students as outright adversaries, we often do classify them according to a deficit mindset. Faculty discourse tends to be very cognizant of what our students *can't* do—*they can't write; they don't know any math*—and remarkably inattentive to what they *can* do. As a result, the dominant pedagogy of higher education has become the lecture, or some close variant, where an expert holds power over the learning space and its occupants, the students, are there solely to receive the content. It's pedagogy firmly of a piece with the deficit mindset: if students need something they don't have but that we possess—competence, expertise, credentials—then education is simply a matter of transferring our content to them. The more thoroughly and efficiently we make that transfer, this line of thought goes, the better. For us and our students, both our goals and our roles are clearly defined.

The Brazilian educator and thinker Paulo Freire had a name for this approach to teaching and learning: "the banking concept" of education. In this mode of pedagogy, teaching was reduced to the simple act of "depositing" information and content into students, to be "withdrawn" at some later juncture (an examination, perhaps). After this transactional cycle, whatever was "learned" simply disappeared; it was no longer necessary after being withdrawn and used. These results, of course, aren't anything that resembles actual, meaningful learning. We have research that convincingly shows, however, that this is precisely what occurs throughout much of what is called "learning" in higher education. Numerous studies on learning loss have shown that unless learners have regular opportunities to revisit and apply specific course content, they will forget most of that content (some studies put the proportion at nearly 75 percent!) within three years of having taken a course.[3] This, of course, raises an important question: if students are forgetting most of the content upon which we so obsessively dwell, then what are we really accomplishing? I would offer a different question for us to consider, though: what proportion of these courses is framed by a pedagogy that resembles Freire's banking concept? If we use a pedagogical model intent on merely transferring content to students, and we know from the research that retention of that content over the long term is iffy at best, then our model is unsustainable. Worse, it is actively harming our students and, by extension, higher education writ large.

The banking concept is, to appropriate the metaphor's language, bankrupt. It sends us on a fool's errand, a quixotic attempt to beat the clock as we cram content into students' brains and hope it sticks there until graduation. That's certainly no way to construct a meaningful education. While that seems bad enough, the worst feature of the banking concept approach to pedagogy is that it is fundamentally dehumanizing, and robs both us and our students of the opportunity to construct an educational experience that's transformational, as opposed to simply transactional. As Freire put it, "the banking concept regards men as adaptable, manageable beings. The more students work at storing the deposits entrusted to them, the less they develop the critical consciousness which would result from their intervention in the world as transformers of that world." This erosion of critical faculties serves to "minimize or annul the students' creative power and to stimulate their credulity."[4]

The result of this insidious process is death by pedagogy. That's not hyperbolic: what gives education vitality—critical thinking, exploration, creativity, play, the construction of knowledge—is snuffed out by the banking model of pedagogy. In theory, at least, we conceive of higher education as a space in which students can not only transform themselves but also gather the ideas and tools with which they will transform society. "These graduates will change the world" may be a commencement-day cliché, but it's repeated so often because it captures what we hope will be the outcome of our work with and among our students. Educational practice conducted along the lines of the banking model, though, leaves no room for this type of transformation. Rather, it merely reinforces the sociopolitical and economic structures already in place, structures that operate for the benefit of the few at the expense of the many—something many of our students are all too aware of. Moreover, "implicit in the banking concept," as Freire elaborates, "is the assumption of a dichotomy between human beings and the world: a person is merely *in* the world, not *with* the world . . . he or she is rather the possessor of . . . an empty 'mind' passively open to the reception of deposits of reality from the world outside."[5] In other words, this pedagogical approach does not recognize student agency; learners have no self-efficacy, but rather wait until they are told by someone else "what matters" and what to do with it. The implications of this approach to students and their learning are chilling. Again, Freire's words vividly make the point:

> It follows logically from the banking notion of consciousness that the educator's role is to regulate the way the world "enters into" the students. The teacher's task is to organize a process which already occurs spontaneously, to "fill" the students by making deposits of information which he or she considers to constitute true knowledge. And since people "receive" the world as passive entities, education should make them more passive still, and adapt them to the world. The educated individual is the adapted person, because she or he is better "fit" for the world. Translated into practice, this concept is well suited to the purposes of oppressors, whose tranquility rests on how well people fit the world the oppressors have created, and how little they question it.[6]

If the term "oppressors" seems overwrought, consider the oppression visited upon much of our society by structures and practices of racism, misogyny, and poverty. Then consider how those structures will simply reproduce themselves for a new generation if we do not actively intervene in that process to disrupt—and ultimately prevent—this reproduction. If we want to teach with hope for a better world, we have to reject this stultifying model of pedagogy for our own practice and actively work against it in our institutional environments as well.

This advocacy—think of it as pedagogy for a better world—will almost certainly meet resistance. Some students will push back when they're asked to do things that they don't associate with what learning should be: *Why are we teaching each other? Isn't it your job to do this?* It will chafe colleagues and administrators because it violates the "agreements" that undergird the status quo. What Freire describes as a student "adapted to the world," for example, is different than what most of our institutions call the job-ready, marketable graduate with the requisite "twenty-first-century skills" that employers want. The "regulation" of "how the world enters into our students" that Freire criticizes is for far too many college and university classes the implicit norm for instruction. In an irony that would be amusing were it not so maddening, we (speaking broadly) are often the architects of our own frustrations. Students narrowly focused on GPAs and careerism? Students who are reluctant to critically engage texts, ideas, or issues? Maybe they've internalized what a set of learning environments fashioned along the lines of the banking concept has told them is important. At the same time that we complain about those student behaviors, we may also be teaching in ways that inscribe them as norms for the next set of students.

Developing Our Praxis

So what's the alternative? What does it look like to create environments that humanize instead of dehumanize students, teaching, and learning? This, I think, is the pivotal question behind the ethic of teaching with radical hope. Higher education at its best is an emancipatory, democratizing "practice of freedom" (to use bell hooks's term).[7] Our principal task, then, is to make those aspirations operational, render them tangible in our classrooms and on our campuses. Critical theorists (including Freire) refer to this as *praxis*: the bridging of theory and practice to effect change. In Freire's formulation, praxis is "reflection and action directed at the structures to be transformed."[8] In our everyday routine on campus, in our classrooms and offices and common spaces, with and among our students, that praxis can adopt a myriad of specific forms. Often, in fact, it may look decidedly unspectacular. Grand theoretical pronouncements about radical change are not self-actualizing; they depend upon everyday actions and decisions for efficacy. Too many times, pedagogical theory seems to focus on philosophical and attitudinal shifts while leaving the application portion unsaid. As Maryellen Weimer wrote in *Learner-Centered Teaching*, "if we continue to feed the interest in learning with nothing more than rhetoric, it will not flourish and grow into better instructional practice."[9] For most of us, though, the crucial ingredient is *precisely* that instructional practice. What does a critical and inclusive approach to pedagogy look like with a 4–4 or 5–5 course load? How can we put those principles into practice if we're teaching a full semester's schedule—but it's at three different institutions? How might a graduate student or early career academic embrace a pedagogy of radical hope in the absence of the stability and protections afforded to more privileged sectors of the academy? The answer to these and similar questions lies in our everyday practice.

At the fundamental level, teaching with radical hope is the sum total of the decisions, both routine and exceptional, we make about the learning environments we create and the students with whom we share them. This chapter and the one before it have stressed the importance of how we decide to talk (in the most expansive sense of the term) to and with our students. The messages we convey, whether intentional or not, are products of the decisions we've made (also intentional or not) about how we conduct our educational practice. How we have chosen to conceive of student learning, the ways in which we've selected to conduct our in-class interactions with them and with the course material—these too have important implications for our overall practice. In subsequent chapters, we'll see how even the seemingly quotidian and decidedly unspectacular choices involved in things like policy statements in our syllabi, or how we approach the use of technology in the classroom, are components of our praxis, and ought to be conceived as such.

This praxis is grounded in an ethic of radical hope first and foremost simply because we engage in it. If we *didn't* think what we were doing with and among our students mattered, if we knew our actions had no impact on shaping a more just and humane future through our students, then we wouldn't be doing it. It's that simple. We certainly wouldn't be making the sacrifices—everything from shitty job markets, low wages, and contingent contracts to public and political scorn—to continue teaching if we felt that way. In that sense, our very perseverance, with the accompanying imperative to do what we do thoughtfully and skillfully, is an expression of a truly radical hope.

To teach, and to care about doing it well enough and in a way that's just, equitable, and humane for our students and our communities, is a radical stance. It is both a statement of fundamental principles and a counternarrative to the neoliberal stories of resource cutting, declines, and deficits that suffuse higher education. Again, however, that stance has to be more than proclamations; it has to be actionable in every space within the wide variety of teaching and learning environments in which we might find ourselves. Let's now turn to some of the specific sets of choices we can make about those learning environments: how we shape them for our students, and how we and our students move together within them.

INTO PRACTICE

Consider keeping a "time journal" of several class sessions with your students; break your class period into five-minute "chunks" and record what you spend the majority of each chunk doing. Alternatively, you might consider video-recording a class session (if your campus has a teaching and learning center, its staff will likely be able to do this for you) and using the recording to log your time. As you look at this specific breakdown of what you're doing with class time, ask yourself: How much time do you spend in instructor-centered methods (e.g., lecturing) and how much time do you spend using student-centered methods of instruction (e.g., discussion, group work, peer instruction)? What trends do you observe in your teaching, and do they align with your broader pedagogical philosophy?

For a variation of this time-journaling exercise, consider writing a brief journal entry that discusses how you allocate the time in a typical class session and contains your best guess as to what each five-minute chunk would look like. Then do the journaling or recording discussed above and compare the results with your predictions. Do they match, or is there a difference between how you remembered class time being used and what the actual record showed was the case? Then consider some of the ways in which you can more closely align specific instructional methods with your larger philosophical goals for student learning.

—

CHAPTER 4

TEACHING AND LEARNING INCLUSIVELY

—

As part of my course rotation, I regularly offer an upper-level course on the US Civil War and Reconstruction eras. It's a reading- and writing-intensive class, and I ask students to read six or seven scholarly monographs and a wide range of documents and other primary sources during the semester. I had a core handful of monographs that I assigned, and rotated a few others in and out depending upon what the latest scholarship was, or if an edition became available in paperback. I felt like I curated a good set of readings as I taught the course over repeated iterations; I employed a raft of prizewinning books (including a Pulitzer) which collectively embodied a variety of scholarly approaches to the eras.

A few years ago, however, I read an excellent blog post by the Civil War historian Megan Kate Nelson, a scholar for whom I have tremendous respect, on the gender bias that pervades academics' networks on social media.[1] In particular, Nelson pointed out that male scholars' work (both formal and informal) was circulated, promoted, retweeted, and "liked" far more than female scholars' work was. As I read the piece, I wondered how much of that effect was present in the ways in which scholarship is perhaps most extensively "promoted": course assignments. I was teaching the Civil War and Reconstruction course at the time, so I mentally scanned the list of books I'd assigned for my students. To my surprise and chagrin, they were all authored by white men, senior scholars who (with one exception) were professors at elite universities: the very definition of "the grand old men" of the field. Moreover, I had apparently never thought hard enough about those readings to realize this uniformity existed. In and of itself, this wouldn't be a terrible thing, perhaps, but I'd structured my course around the theme of the diversity of historical experience. Harping on this theme, I repeatedly exhorted my students to make sure they were paying attention to as many historical perspectives as they could (including the dispossessed and marginalized). But now I realized that my assigned materials were murmuring a dissenting narrative against the main theme of the course, and wondered how much cognitive dissonance had been created as a result. Clearly, I thought, I needed to revisit the thought process that produced my required course reading list.

I didn't need to wait long. A scheduling quirk allowed me the opportunity to teach the same course again the next semester, as part of a consortium in which my university was participating. Taking my cue from Nelson's essay and the thinking it sparked about how I was representing the scholarship of this particular subfield to my students, I completely revamped my reading list. Every monograph I assigned was by a female scholar. I wanted to emphasize gender in particular; Civil War history (particularly the era's military history) had long been a male-dominated field, but that has been changing dramatically over the last twenty years. I wanted my course to reflect this trend in the scholarship. I didn't tell my students, or emphasize the course readings any differently just because they were all authored by women (plus, I was curious to see if anyone actually noticed).

As it turned out, no one in the class, which was about evenly split between men and women, remarked upon the gendered nature of the reading list. The semester went well, as I had a remarkably engaged group of students. But it was the course evaluations that surprised me. In my fifteen or so years of teaching this course, I could count the number of students who'd actually used the course evaluation to offer an opinion about the readings on one hand (and those were complaints about the *amount* of reading more than anything). But for this iteration, *every student* commented (without any prompting on my part) about the books for the course: they liked the books, they found the reading fascinating, they were surprised by the different methods and perspectives the authors brought to the period, the books were different than the muskets-and-bugles battlefield histories they had expected. Every student had something to say, and it was positive.

To be sure, this is anecdotal data, but I took important lessons from it. First, being intentional about including perspectives that aren't the dominant voices in a scholarly field ensures that I don't just tell students there's a diversity of approaches to the subject; rather, I can show them that's the case and invite them to experience some of those approaches for themselves. Second, in ensuring that my course materials represented a diversity of scholars—in this case, women (about half of whom were also women of color)—I was able to present my students with an array of knowledge producers much more representative of the current state of the field.

Finally, I also concluded that this experiment led me to choose not just different, but *better* materials. I'd gotten comfortable with some of the "greatest hits" of the literature, and hadn't paid enough attention to incorporating some of the new scholarly perspectives that were making waves and shaping the current discourse. As a result, I had been selling my students *and* my discipline short. By selecting materials with an eye toward diversifying the scholarly voices my students would encounter, I was being more intentional about encountering different perspectives—which was, after all, one of the touchstone themes around which I'd built the course!

In subsequent iterations of this class, the reading list has shifted a bit. Some male scholars are present, though the monographs still lean female. The primary source documents are as accurate a cross section of American society in the mid-nineteenth century as I can manage. I've reaped substantial benefits from this retooled approach to selecting course materials. Perhaps most essentially, I no longer worry about my course materials undermining my larger message about critically engaging with different viewpoints. I am ensuring that the diversity of my field is reflected in how that field is encountered by my students. I am providing my students with meaningful examples of how people like them engage in the scholarly work of history, as well as how people like them in the past reckoned with that history as it unfolded. In short, I am creating a much better climate in which my students and I can do the type of heavy lifting a course like this requires: rigorous analysis of differing perspectives; tracing and critiquing an unfamiliar or innovative argument; and understanding how history is not just "what happened," but the product of conversations and debates among historians. In the end, a decision about what books to use ended up having exponentially larger consequences for my course, and for the community of students who entered that learning space, than I could have guessed. I was striving for inclusivity, but I got that and a lot more.

Why Inclusion Matters

What does it mean to teach inclusively? What is involved in an inclusive pedagogy? And why do the identities of the authors of my required texts matter, anyway? The short answer is there are many areas in which our students' lived experience is one of exclusion. Students from under-resourced school districts, students of color, LGBTQIA students, students from non-Christian faith traditions—there are a number of ways in which our society excludes people from nonmajority and nondominant groups. This exclusion can take its toll in virtually every aspect—both affective and cognitive—of one's day-to-day life, a hard truth to which many of our students would attest. There are two clear reasons this exclusionary climate is an urgent problem for us in higher education. First, the effect on those students' academic performance is profound; the amount of cognitive bandwidth taken up by navigating the treacherous terrain of a world that sometimes resents your presence can be staggering. And that's bandwidth that can't be devoted to things like study, analysis, or reading beyond the superficial level.[2] Second, higher education proclaims itself to be the arena of opportunity and the engine driving the changes necessary to create a better world. We say the education we offer possesses urgent importance and relevance. We claim institutions of higher education are an inherent good for our society and polity. But institutional and educational practices that exclude students—that push them to the margins, figuratively or literally—render those pronouncements nothing more than a cruel joke. We may not be able to control the factors that shape our students' experiences outside of our classrooms, but we have a great deal of control over the climate within that space. We should absolutely use that power to make the types of decisions that create a welcoming and inclusive climate. It's a fairly easy proposition to create a course in which a certain type of student can succeed. It's much more difficult to create one in which there is equitable opportunity for all of our students to succeed.

All of us have a favorite type of student, one that demonstrates certain habits or aptitudes we find attractive: the student who writes brilliantly, the usually quiet student who will occasionally offer the type of thoughtful and perceptive comment that transforms a discussion, the student who comes to office hours because they want to know more about the topic covered in class. There's nothing wrong with that, but we need to guard against creating learning spaces that we subconsciously shape for that preferred type of student at the expense of the actual diversity of learners we are certain to encounter. When I was an undergraduate history major, I was enthralled by witty and erudite lectures delivered by venerable professors. I sat in the front row for these classes, listened eagerly, and took extensive notes (this was certainly not typical behavior for much of the rest of my undergraduate experience, it should be pointed out). But now that I'm teaching my own courses, I can't just teach to the newer versions of motivated undergraduate me; I need to teach to the present-day versions of the students who were sitting behind me in those classes, too. In my experience, attempting to duplicate witty, erudite lectures was a profound pedagogical failure. I've been much more successful in my teaching by conceiving my approach in broader terms. If we are calibrating our course design and pedagogy toward some ideal student archetype, then we are deciding to exclude any students who don't fit that mold. That decision is no less powerful or self-evident for its being implicit, either. Those students, who don't align with that archetype, looking into a class that they are *in*, but not *of*, will certainly be aware that decision has been made.

If we want to say to each one of our students, *you are welcome here, and you can succeed*, then it's incumbent upon us to create inclusive learning spaces. As Frank Tuitt observes, we have to not only design our pedagogy for a greater diversity of students but also create learning environments "which respect and care for the souls of our students."[3] That phrase, "care for the souls of our students," might seem outside the bounds of our everyday discourse about teaching and learning, but I would submit that this type of care is an integral part of a genuinely effective pedagogy. It's not a demand that we become students' spiritual advisors or therapists, but rather that we simply see them as full and complicated human beings, just as we ourselves are. In doing so, we can then discern the ways in which our learning environments can be a place of radical welcome and maximum inclusion. We can understand that our students have taken many different paths to arrive in our classroom, and the fact that those paths have converged with ours doesn't mean they lose any of their salience. Some of our students arrive having been less than successful in previous attempts at our disciplines, or maybe even in our specific course. Others carry with them a belief that they have something inherently "wrong," that people like them aren't supposed to be successful in the particular area we're teaching. Some are the first in their families to pursue higher education and are unsure what to expect. Others might be dealing with financial precarity, food insecurity, family or personal trauma, or academic unpreparedness. As the number of students enrolled in postsecondary institutions remains near historically high levels, and the diversity within that student body grows even more complex, our awareness of—and solicitude for—these different types of paths will only have to become sharper.

As we confront this bewildering array of considerations, faculty tend to respond in one of two ways. One is to shut out the noise, to act as if our class space somehow exists outside the larger context of both our institutions and society and that students walk into it out of a vacuum. Course content is what matters; the rest is meaningless, at least for the time we and our students are in class. The other type of response is to acknowledge this increasingly difficult terrain and design our learning spaces with that in mind—spaces where course content is important but the learners are more so. The first option is an easy one to default into; *on top of all the other things that go into our faculty responsibilities, in addition to the numerous problems with which we're already struggling, now we need to rethink our course design and pedagogy so that we can coddle our students? In my day, we toughed it out and focused on our studies no matter what other distractions tried to derail us.* That may be true in some of our personal stories, but our students are not us. There may be more demands being placed upon us than before, but effective teaching and the promotion of student learning have always been paramount. That's why we must choose the second option. If we want our students to learn, we have to pay attention to all of the things that either assist in or interfere with that learning. Some of the obstacles to learning are specific to our course spaces, but many are not. If we understand that our students' paths into our course may have placed some barriers in the way of effective learning, we can anticipate some of them as we design and implement our courses. We know that students learn better when they are actively included, feel valued as members of the class community, and see what they're learning as relevant to them personally, and we ought to be designing course spaces where those features figure prominently—even if that means significant changes to our own practice. This "learner-centered teaching" thing may sound like a simple thing to adopt, but "simple" doesn't always mean "easy." To teach all of the students we have, it's vital for us to both implicitly and explicitly foster an atmosphere of inclusion.

Creating Inclusive Learning Spaces

Creating an inclusive climate begins even in the seemingly innocuous, quotidian choices we make about things such as what textbooks to adopt. The selection of course materials may occur without much thought at all; perhaps the department uses a standard text for all sections of a particular course, perhaps there's a book you've used ever since the first time you taught this particular course, perhaps you got a cool desk copy from a publisher's representative, or perhaps you eschew textbooks altogether. For others, the selection of course materials is a painstaking and thorough process where the list gets whittled down by paying attention to such factors as pedagogical fit, coverage of what you see as the most important content areas, theoretical currency, or monetary cost to students. But rarely do we see inclusion as part of this criteria. A simple thought experiment might help underscore its importance, however: if you were a newcomer to your discipline, and only had the list of course materials on your syllabus (textbooks, other readings, videos, anything students will be using to access information) to go by, who would you see as the creators of knowledge in your discipline? Chances are, the list produced by this exercise tilts heavily toward both the monochromatic and male, as the reading list for my Civil War and Reconstruction course once did. If we were not so well versed in our disciplines and engaged in their conversations and debates, this exercise would give us a remarkably narrow conception of who the movers and shakers in the particular field are. Yet that is precisely the situation for our students: the materials we put in front of them, materials we are likely requiring them to use, are for most of them the first glimpse of the "face of our discipline." The textbook authors, or experts in videos, or examples in the case studies: these are the people who we hold up as the experts who produce knowledge for, and who participate in the scholarly conversations within, our disciplines. However, I would lay odds that there are significant numbers of our students who do not see themselves in that category, as people who could actually produce knowledge or participate in the scholarly conversation. For much, if not all, of their academic careers, many of our students have not seen themselves reflected in the course materials they are required to use. Perhaps this is one of the underappreciated explanations for the difficulties we sometimes encounter with unmotivated students.

How do we make our selection of materials more inclusive, and more importantly, a better reflection of the diversity of learners who will engage in our courses? Put simply, representation matters. Critics of this idea will immediately assume I'm advocating some sort of racial and gender quota system, but that's not the case at all. Making course materials genuinely representative is a necessary practice for reasons that embrace both student motivation and fidelity to our disciplines. To begin with, we know that students learn better when they are positively motivated to do so. There are a number of factors that increase student motivation, but one of the more important is "value"; that is, do students see the value of the course and what they are being asked to do within it? For example, a student who sees the course material as directly bearing upon her choice of career (e.g., it will help her pass a licensure exam) will approach the course with a higher degree of motivation. Even in courses that may not have such an explicit quid pro quo, we can still increase student motivation by making it possible for students to see some part of themselves or their identities within the "knowledge" they encounter. If students see people who look or talk like them, or are in some other ways reflective of their identity or experience, then they attach a significant degree of value to that content.[4] More importantly, they can be empowered by that suggestion of agency to see themselves as active participants, rather than passive observers, in the explication and analysis of that particular material.

This empowerment is also an important safeguard against some of the processes, such as stereotype threat, that work against the motivation and performance of students of color. For example, the prominent narrative in most STEM disciplines is one that does not generally include African American or Latinx people, especially judging by the so-called leaky pipeline that accounts for these groups being significantly underrepresented in the ranks of PhD programs or the professoriate in STEM fields. Coupled with the socioeconomic discrimination that steers many students from these groups into underperforming secondary schools, and thus most often into remedial and developmental college math courses, this demographic reality would make it easy for an African American or Latinx student to assume that math—and perhaps science as well—is not an area where "people like me" do well. But what if the course materials included diverse authors? What if the problem sets used names and cultural references that drew them closer to the lived experiences of *all* students? Even seemingly minor adjustments like this would go far in neutralizing the pernicious narratives that undergird so much of stereotype threat's observed effects.[5]

Yet, as powerful as these factors are, the argument for inclusive course materials doesn't end there. Selecting and framing course materials and activities with inclusion in mind also maximizes the odds of reflecting our discipline's complex content and conversations accurately. None of our disciplines looks like the monochromatic male rosters of the "classic" textbook authors. To rely on such a narrow sub-segment of our disciplines elides much of the richness and kaleidoscopic diversity of thought within them. In my home discipline of history, for example, there's been a veritable explosion of different modes of thought, argument, and analysis produced by an ever-increasing variety of scholars over the last few decades, a phenomenon that is only accelerating. What good would be served by preventing my students from seeing that swirling complexity in action?

Moving Students from the Margins to the Center

All this being said, it's important to emphasize that adding diverse course materials without taking corresponding steps to render the rest of our course environment more inclusive is a pedagogical misstep. It's all too easy to congratulate ourselves for rethinking the materials we use while otherwise retaining the same patterns and structures in the rest of our course design and classroom practice. There is always the danger (especially for those of us who are white) that we do just enough diversity work to convince ourselves we've done enough, and duck the harder questions of equity and justice with which we need to engage. The critical theorist Herbert Marcuse called this "repressive tolerance," describing situations in which just enough dissent against the status quo is permitted in order to allow individuals upholding that status quo to claim they are tolerant of other viewpoints without actually having to do anything of substance.[6] Stephen Brookfield and Stephen Preskill discuss how problematic repressive tolerance can be in an educational setting:

> When they experience repressive tolerance . . . people mistakenly believe they are participating in discussions characterized by freedom of speech and an inclusive emphasis on diverse ideas, when in fact those same discussions actually reinforce dominant ideology. Repressive tolerance is a tolerance for just enough challenge to an unjust system to convince people that they live in a truly open society in which dissenting voices are expressed and heard. As long as people believe this, they will lose the energy to try and change the system, even though in reality nothing has altered.[7]

If we merely proclaim an openness to previously marginalized perspectives without doing the work to bring those perspectives from the margins to the center, then our efforts are incomplete. Moreover, we are letting ourselves and our students down. Choosing course materials while asking "who creates knowledge in this field?" is thoughtful practice; choosing course materials to check off boxes on some arbitrary list of "different identities" is missing the point. The former begins a much deeper conversation about inclusion and learning spaces; the latter replaces that conversation with a shallow performative "wokeness." To invest in creating a truly inclusive learning space is to commit to a process, an evolving pedagogical worldview as opposed to a discrete set of techniques. Sure, there are specific actions that we can—and should—consider taking, like reenvisioning the ways we select and implement course materials and assignments. But there is a whole that is greater than the sum of these parts, and we should keep that in the foreground.

This is why creating inclusive learning spaces is an integral part of teaching from a place of radical hope. If we believe that higher education is an essential part of creating a better future for all, then it behooves us to do everything we can to help ensure that this better future *for* all is actively shaped *by* all. The benefits of higher education are numerous and complex, and they also unfold over time. In order for those benefits to be scaled to a societal level, we must make a collective effort to include all of our students in the process by which they can access them. That means we have to pay more attention to things like inclusivity, motivation, and values. The revolution is in the details.

We must pay close attention to who our students *really* are. Social and cultural identities have so often been weaponized against students' educational opportunities, and we need to understand just how much that has affected them prior to arriving on our campus. A critically inclusive pedagogical approach is vital to ensuring that all of our students have both meaningful access and opportunities to learn. Most colleges and universities have a range of programs for "culturally diverse" students: clubs and organizations, multicultural centers, and the like. These are valuable experiences, and of clear benefit to students. However, there's a definite limit to their impact if our extra- and co-curricular attention to diverse student needs is not accompanied by attention to curricular inclusive teaching and learning. Too often, we convince ourselves that having diversity programs is enough, something the student affairs people do, and don't examine what's happening in the classroom and other academic spaces (either physical or online)—which are, after all, the very heart of our students' academic journeys. Moreover, as Sara Ahmed has incisively argued, sometimes diversity language actually undercuts meaningful inclusivity. Institutions can often point to their oft-stated commitments to diversity (in things like strategic plans and admissions materials) as evidence they're "diverse," and at the same time not do the work to implement the measures necessary for a genuinely inclusive campus environment. Abstract, theoretical claims of diversity often mask practices that are racist, sexist, or perpetuate other types of inequities.[8] To work against this sort of institutional and pedagogical complacency, we have to practice ways of being with our students that recognize and value their identities and experiences.

The Challenges to Inclusive Pedagogy

The critics of this type of recognition and affirmation (and there are many) tend to characterize it as "dumbing down" college, as some sort of hippy-dippy "identity politics" that focuses on making students feel good instead of challenging them. The implication here is that an inclusive climate is somehow antithetical to academic rigor, that truly intellectual activities can only take place in an environment of individuated competition and argumentation, where reason and facts reign supreme over feelings and emotions. In other words, an inclusive approach to pedagogy appears to threaten the basic "agreements" (to again use Laura Rendón's description) some see as essential to the enterprise of higher education. This line of criticism is emblematic of a larger disdain for, or anxiety about, the work involved in committing to a pedagogy of radical hope. A criticism of inclusive pedagogy that assumes it dumbs things down is an implicit attack on the capabilities and faculties of students of color or students from other marginalized groups. A criticism of inclusive pedagogy that caricatures it as an exclusively affective set of practices posits an artificial distinction between the realms of cognition and emotion, one that flies in the face of what we know from the research.[9] These criticisms privilege a view of student-faculty relationships that is hierarchical and often adversarial, rather than collaborative and trusting. We cannot embrace a pedagogy of radical hope if we implement practices based in pessimistic cynicism.

So how do we answer those criticisms, then? How does one rebut the veteran member of the department who's had decades to hone his disdain for "touchy-feely stuff" such as active learning or inclusive teaching? There are a number of ways to go about doing so, but their viability very much depends on our own position—tenured or not, full-time or adjunct, faculty or grad student. We should ask ourselves if the conversation will be one that has consequences, or if it's one where we can count on our interlocutor's good faith. It does us no good to defend a pedagogical outlook by fruitlessly diverting emotional and intellectual energy away from its practice. Some hills are just not worth dying on. In my experience, the most effective way to address the critics of inclusive pedagogy is with competence and results. There is a wealth of research supporting specific approaches that inhere in an inclusive approach to pedagogy. Evidence-based practices stand on pretty firm ground, especially if the result is demonstrable improvements in student learning.[10]

It's worth acknowledging these criticisms and their sway in some quarters of higher education, because it underscores the necessity of committing to the work in order for it to be successful for our students and their learning. Inclusive pedagogy is hard work indeed, not least because it asks us to honestly and critically reflect on our own assumptions and practices. Sometimes the results of this critically reflective practice are not ones we're very happy about. As Stephen Brookfield writes, "we are all prisoners in the perceptual frameworks that determine how we view our experiences."[11] And just as students struggle with the challenges to their established worldview presented by pivotal episodes in their college education, so too do we ourselves struggle to reckon with the ways in which we are products of systems and structures that can work at cross-purposes with our professed philosophies. None of us likes to admit we did things unskillfully or just plain wrong. My teaching career is littered with episodes of maladroit practice that still cause me to cringe years later; sometimes, self-assessment and self-correction suck. But this kind of reflection shouldn't be simply an exercise in self-flagellation; we should be generous with ourselves in the same ways we are with students when the occasion calls for it. Many of us weren't trained for this in our graduate work, after all. In fact, for many of us, our graduate training—at the same time it essentially ignored pedagogy—was also conditioning us to become an expert on whatever showed up on our intellectual radar screen and hence to judge our worth on the degree of said expertise we were able to profess. Yet, we also came to realize just how difficult it is to actually command a subject and acquire legit-imate expertise. The tension that comes from holding these two ideas simultaneously is why impostor syndrome is very much a real thing, and endemic in academia. It's also why we can struggle to be critically reflective practitioners when it comes to our pedagogy; we have to admit to ourselves that we aren't experts, that there are areas of our practice where we need work and even where we've made mistakes. And that means we have to become vulnerable to our harshest critic: ourselves. Teaching is an endeavor that's often tightly intertwined with our own professional and scholarly identities, and to make it an object of critical reflection is to venture into risky territory indeed. That's precisely why we need to engage in this type of self-work, though. If we think the stakes are high for ourselves, consider what they are for our students.

INTO PRACTICE

Perform the thought experiment discussed earlier in this chapter: if your syllabi were all someone had to go by, how would they describe the knowledge creators of your particular field or discipline? Consider scaling the experiment up: using all the syllabi for multiple sections of a particular course, perhaps, or even the syllabi for an entire department. What is the aggregate portrait of your field's scholarly conversations, as conveyed by this larger data set? Does that portrait reflect the goals of the curriculum or program? If not, what are the tangible steps you can take to name and address this misalignment?

Consider a journal entry or freewrite that takes as its subject one of your current course sections, and list every form of student diversity within that section you can think of. Next, consider how many "invisible" elements of diversity might be present as well. Finally, consider the ways in which your students might be standing at the intersections of two, three, or several of these forms of diversity, and what that means for the ways they are experiencing the learning environment. In what ways might your course be (re)considered as a more inclusive space for *all* of your students?

CHAPTER 5

MAKING ACCESS MEAN SOMETHING

When I facilitate workshops with college teachers, I like to do an exercise that underscores the effects of climate on student learning. I ask everyone to take out a piece of paper and something to write with, and inform them we're going to do a timed—and graded—writing exercise. Then I give them the instructions: when I put the prompt up on the screen, they will have two minutes to write as much of an answer as they can. The only stipulation is that they must use their *left* hand to complete the exercise. (*What if we're left-handed?* someone usually asks; I simply repeat the instructions to use their left hand.) The prompt I give covers a lot of ground, and is always open ended; typically, it's something along the lines of "What is the most important element of your pedagogical philosophy, and why?" You know, something plenty easy to describe in two minutes using, most likely, your nondominant hand (given that only about 10 percent of the population is left-handed).

The next two minutes are filled with exasperated sighs, chuckles, a hum of sometimes frustrated conversation, and the few left-handers in the group snickering to themselves as they write ten words for every one their neighbor is able to scratch out. Once the time has elapsed, I ask the participants to exchange papers with their neighbors so we can grade the work. Then I put up the grading criteria: fifty points for penmanship and fifty points for word count, for a total of 100 points. I also stipulate there must be at least forty words for the writer to receive credit for their word count—any less than forty, no points given. As you might imagine, these criteria do not go over well. So I explain to the group that there is, in fact, a well-considered rationale for these standards. Clarity of expression is an essential basis for effective communication, I tell them, so penmanship is important. Besides, don't we always harp on how our students should learn to write as neatly as we did when we were in school? Here's your chance to put those principles into practice! For the word count, I explain that it's an important skill to be able to distill complex ideas and analyses into concise and accessible language, yet still be able to convey something of substance. And for such a weighty subject as one's pedagogical philosophy, I conclude, surely there ought to be at least forty words; heck, that's just a few lines of text, after all!

Having thoroughly annoyed most of the group by this point, I make that annoyance complete by following through on my threat to have them grade each other's work. It doesn't take very long, because almost no one gets above a 50 out of 100. I know how we academics are wired, and even though this is a somewhat silly exercise whose points literally do not matter, most of the folks in the room are in a state ranging from bemused to exasperated to (in the occasional case) straight-up angry. When I ask for a show of hands from the people who actually passed, there are never more than a few, and they have always been the left-handers in the room. When I solicit descriptions of how the participants felt when I unveiled the grading criteria, the reactions are also pretty consistent. *I thought it was a joke; I couldn't believe we were going to use criteria that are this unrealistic/meaningless/ unfair/dumb; I was already frustrated, and these standards made it worse.*

At this point, the method to my seemingly arbitrary madness comes into sharper focus. When I ask what was pedagogically wrong with this "assignment," there is no shortage of opinions on the matter because, of course, I did pretty much everything wrong by design. I gave a writing prompt that required a fair amount of thought and explanation in order to do well, and imposed an unreasonably brief time limit in which to write. I imposed arbitrary conditions for the completion of the assignment, and these conditions did not operate equally—some were advantaged (shout-out to the left-handers) and others had a significant obstacle placed in their path. Moreover, it was unclear how (or even if) these conditions had any bearing on the assignment or its purpose; what does pedagogical philosophy have to do with which hand one uses to write? Adding insult to injury, the criteria were skewed towards those who had been advantaged by the conditions in which the assignment was completed; those who already wrote with their left hand had no problem meeting the minimum word count, while few of those using their nondominant hand came close to that threshold—and thus instantly lost half of the assignment's possible points. Even though this activity was introduced as a graded assignment, the criteria weren't made available before the group was asked to begin writing, so they could only guess at how they would be assessed. Finally, and perhaps most egregiously, the criteria were only tangentially related to the actual task the participants were asked to complete. For all my pontificating about the importance of clear communication and the ability to express complex thoughts in a brief period of time, what I was really asking these "students" to do was write about pedagogy. Yet they were being assessed on seemingly everything *but* that. They could have written "All work and no play makes Jack a dull boy" in neat script enough times to meet the word count and gotten a hundred out of a hundred points.

"Yeah, but other than all that, though, this is a well-designed assignment," I protest. That line usually gets a good laugh or two, but the laughter stops when I ask the next question: *how many of our students experience college this way?* When it comes to one of the most important elements of an inclusive pedagogical approach—*access*—the answer is unfortunately "too many by far." Yet access is one of the most prominent words in our current discourse surrounding higher education. Who has access to college, and how? How does access to higher education vary depending upon such variables as socioeconomic status? The range of proposals for free college (most often, these are calls for tuition subsidization) trumpets increasing college access as one of its main benefits. There may be the occasional "some kids aren't ready for college" codicil brought up from time to time, but there seems to be a broad consensus that access is a good thing, and ought to be expanded. To adopt a pedagogy based in radical hope is to be pro-access as well; if higher education is indeed the social and political good we believe it is, then we should be doing our level best to ensure as many students as possible are able to access the opportunity to pursue it.

However, when we talk about access in higher education, it's important to ask ourselves precisely what we believe students should have access *to*. Increasing access is a laudable goal, but only if we mean students should be able to access the types of resources that allow them to fashion their own academic success. Access is nothing but a cruel joke if we simply define it as allowing students in the front door and then letting them drift through campus and curricula as they may. Increasing access to traditionally underrepresented groups is vital, but so too is ensuring that our campuses have the resources and support to make that access actually mean something. When we talk about online learning as increasing access to higher education for more and more learners, that's only a good thing if our online courses do more than just digitally replicate the worst and most unimaginative aspects of face-to-face pedagogy. Moving from the institutional to the individual level, we should be thinking about access as a feature of our own pedagogy. How do we ensure students *access* in our courses? Do all of our students have the same degree of access to us, the course, the material, and to learning?

Universal Design for Learning

If we are going to practice an inclusive pedagogy, accessibility has to be one of the areas to which we pay close attention. If you've taught online, you're likely familiar with some of the specific facets of accessibility simply because of the different demands of an online modality in meeting the needs of different types of learners. Indeed, much of what we see as important in terms of accessibility in our face-to-face teaching was first brought to our collective attention by practitioners of blended and online teaching. This is the case for one of the most important topics in higher education at the moment: the conversation surrounding Universal Design for Learning

(UDL). I first encountered UDL while developing my first online course and was asked to think about how a visually impaired student would navigate the course readings and assignments. At first, I had no answer whatsoever. In doing the work to educate myself, I learned about screen-reader technology, accessible PDFs, and a host of other tools that needed to be in my oeuvre; in the long run, though, that was my introduction to not just the specific practices of UDL, but the larger philosophy upon which it rests. Put simply, UDL asks us to stop thinking about disability and accommodations as somehow deviating from the desired norms for teaching and learning, and instead challenge ourselves to create a learning space that might not need to make accommodations in the first place. Rather than pathologizing and "othering" students with disabilities, can we instead approach our work through a paradigm that allows for diverse ways of learning, and then incorporate that range of difference into our course design and activities? That's how we create learning spaces that serve all of our students well, which is the commitment at the center of teaching from a place of hope.

In designing the spaces in which our students will learn, we must make a fundamental commitment to *equity*. Again, I want to emphasize that equity and equality, while related concepts, are not completely synonymous: treating all of our students exactly the same exacerbates rather than removes systemic inequities. The twenty to thirty percent of our students who have a disability that interferes with their learning understand this point implicitly. This is a significant portion of our students, and the number will only increase over time given the higher rate of diagnoses (and improved understanding) of learning-related disabilities in the K–12 world. Too often, though, working with the diverse ways in which our students learn becomes a conversation simply about disability forms and specific classroom accommodations. One student needs note-taking assistance, another extra time on examinations, and before long (especially in a large class) it becomes nearly impossible to keep up with what arrangements we've made for which students. Even for faculty who consider themselves committed student advocates, the increased workload and bureaucratized processes can lead to frustration that sometimes spills over into interactions with our students. We want to help our students, but also worry about changes to our courses and the appearance of weakening standards. I've had several colleagues over the years tell me they refuse to make accommodations for disabilities because they believe it "lets the student off too easy" and undermines the "rigor" of their courses. This is, of course, an unworkable stance; it penalizes students for faculty anxieties and it's also illegal. But it's reflective of a larger tension that we in higher education must do a better job of addressing. How do we abide by our ethical duty to help students, as well as the obligations of law and institutional policy, to make our learning environments both inclusive and fair?

This is where UDL offers us a set of tools to meet not only the short-term imperatives of our institution's accommodations process, but the more essential obligation to create equitable learning spaces. Let me be clear: I want to advocate for Universal Design for reasons beyond "the law says we have to." That type of reaction-based, formalistic approach runs the risk of making our students feel as if they're imposing on us and somehow stigmatized as a result. Instead, we should embrace UDL as first and foremost a social justice issue. If we want all of our students to have the chance to meaningfully learn, then we need to create a space in which they all can do so—and that means a space characterized by flexibility and options. Almost all of us would argue that teaching is a context-sensitive process, that there is no standard or prefabricated set of principles that define pedagogy. Universal Design for Learning simply asks us to turn this gut feeling into specific practice. As the National Center on Universal Design for Learning describes it, "UDL provides a blueprint for creating instructional goals, methods, materials, and assessments that work for everyone—not a single, one-size-fits-all solution but rather flexible approaches that can be customized and adjusted for individual needs."[1] In practice, this can mean a welter of different things, ranging from providing written transcripts of video materials to formulating several distinct but related pathways for students to complete their assignments. Multiple modalities is the key concept here: practicing the principles of UDL means offering our students "multiple means of engagement, multiple means of representation, and multiple means of action and expression." As Thomas Tobin and Kirsten Behling put it in the title of their excellent overview, UDL allows us to "reach everyone, teach everyone."[2]

I see this as a social justice issue because it's a powerful way for us to include students who have been relegated to the margins of the typical higher education learning environment. If higher education is to be the force for genuine and positive change we want it to be, and that it can be at its best, then we simply cannot allow for *any* of our students to be marginalized. We know that students are often marginalized by race, ethnicity, sexual identity, socioeconomic class, and a number of other factors—indeed, this marginalization often occurs at the intersections of several of these factors in our students' identities. But in an academic environment, the ways in which we structure courses and other learning activities can also push some of our students to the margins as well. It's a more subtle, but just as powerfully alienating, process. Think of the student who is visually impaired and has to constantly request screen-reader-compatible versions of material that other students can simply download from the course website. Think of how that student, every time they do so, wonders whether the instructor even cares enough to realize that what's posted for the class isn't accessible for them? Then think about the energy—the cognitive bandwidth, if you will—that student uses up in what's become a tiresome ritual of simply getting access to the basic materials they need on a day-to-day basis to keep up in the course. The instructor might respond with something like *I'm too busy to format different versions of something that's easily findable online. Do you know how much time it would take to track every article down? I don't even know how I would format a version for screen readers to begin with.* Now imagine how the student *wants* to respond to these excuses: *I'm too busy with a full class load to download every article and reformat it. And I know how much time it takes to track every article down, because I've been doing it all semester. And is it my job to teach you what you're required to do by this university's disabilities policy?* Of course, the actual response by the student will probably be something more along the lines of weary resignation, if they don't drop the class entirely. Here is a student who has been thoroughly marginalized—not by any overt action from the instructor, but rather a series of thoughtless abdications of responsibility and an unwillingness to consider contextual circumstances. They have been denied access to the learning opportunities their peers receive on a regular basis in the same course at the same institution.

There are literally hundreds of examples of the different ways students can be pushed to the margins like this. Most of them have two things in common: the student has been asked to bear an exceptional and unfair share of responsibility for their access to learning, and instructors do not realize that they are playing a central role in marginalizing some of their students (indeed, many would be horrified by this realization). Regardless of intent or awareness, though, the end result is still a fundamentally inequitable learning environment. Universal Design for Learning is an important safeguard against not just pedagogy's sins of omission, but its sins of commission also. Think of a different way the previous scenario could have unfolded: before the semester started, the instructor ensured that course readings were uploaded to the LMS as PDFs formatted for screen readers. The visually impaired student didn't have to spend an inordinate amount of time simply chasing down the material, but instead was able to devote the time and cognitive resources to earn an A in the course. But now, think about some of the other ways in which the instructor's decision might have paid off: the student who has an hour-long bus ride from their job to campus uses their smartphone and a text-reader app to listen to the course readings on their way to class (or even sometimes at their job when things are slow); the student struggling with some of the theoretical language can listen to the articles as they visually follow along with the text. Hell, even the student who wants to get their cardio in at the gym can listen to a PDF narrated to them while they're on the elliptical trainer. A decision by the instructor to address a specific circumstance—in this case, the knowledge one of their students was visually impaired—ended up having positive effects on student learning well beyond the original case. It's one of the few times we can accurately use the old cliché that a rising tide lifts all boats.

The case for accessibility and the arguments for inclusive teaching may have initially focused on particular subsets of students, but they have become so compelling because of their self-evident benefits for the entire student population. The oft-cited example in the UDL literature is curb-cuts, the nearly ubiquitous sidewalk ramps located at intersections. Originally implemented to accommodate wheelchair users, they've proven eminently useful for bicyclists, visually impaired pedestrians, baby strollers, and many others. Now, curb-cuts are such an important and expected environmental feature that we wouldn't pay particular attention to them unless they were absent.[3] So too is UDL a practice that might originally have been aimed at a specific issue, but has proven so beneficial to the entire population that the case for using these principles is an easy one to make. Adjusting our lenses to an even wider angle, we see the same is true for inclusive teaching (the umbrella under which accessibility and other student identity-centered strategies reside). Diversity work aimed at fostering meaningful inclusion has immediate and particular value for our students from marginalized groups. But it also embraces a set of practices that urge our institutions to embrace diversity and inclusion as part of their very DNA, something we know has a significant positive impact on the educational journeys of all our students.[4] There is a wide array, then, of evidence-based practices that resonate with the ideals we seek to advance by teaching from a stance of radical hope.

The Work of Inclusion

But UDL—and, more broadly, inclusive pedagogy—is *hard*. It's *work*. And sometimes, we might feel like we either cannot or don't want to do that work. It can seem overwhelming, contemplating all of these factors to consider in our practice of designing and teaching courses; where does one begin, and how does one proceed coherently? *Sure, I want a more inclusive classroom, but I can't redesign four courses over winter break.* Those with heavy teaching loads (sometimes at multiple institutions), or extensive obligations in areas such as academic advising or institutional service, feel this pressure even more acutely. *How can I make sure all my videos are captioned when I just added another course as overload? What do you mean I need to rethink how I handle group work?* It would be easy to take the off-ramp at this juncture, but it would also be a mistake, one that sells both ourselves and our students short. When we are overwhelmed by the range of possible actions to take and attitudinal and pedagogical shifts to contemplate, it's a good idea to step back and bring some focus to our actions. Ask: *what is the next step*? In other words, you aren't able to embed every UDL practice in each of your courses right now, but you can pick one thing with which to start, then do it. Then, pick another. Rinse, repeat. This is a key part of any effort to keep our practice from going stale in the face of a daunting set of tasks and obstacles.

This consistency in doing *something* is, quite simply, committing to our *praxis*: the combination of reflection and action that constitutes an intervention in the status quo. A praxis grounded in the ethos of radical hope is committed to saying to all of our students *you are valued, you are welcome, we will learn.* It is committed to doing so in ways that aren't patronizing or condescending, but rather effective and empowering. Most essentially, especially for our current moment, it rejects apathy and cynicism. Paulo Freire warned us that "when it becomes a program, hopelessness paralyzes us, immobilizes us. We succumb to fatalism, and then it becomes impossible to muster the strength we absolutely need for a fierce struggle that will re-create the world." If we are committed to teaching, and teaching well, in this higher educational environment, then we are living out a commitment to hope. The alternative, whether it's a product of weary resignation or belligerent cynicism, is to simply go through the motions, to stop doing the work, robbing both ourselves and our students of the opportunities higher education is supposed to embody. Again, Freire sums it up well: "I am hopeful, not out of mere stubbornness, but out of an existential, concrete imperative."[5]

Yet it's easy to lose sight of the practice part of praxis. It's one thing to declare we want to help our students achieve "critical consciousness," to be the architects of their education and, indeed, their reality. But putting that sentiment into actual operation is a complex endeavor, all the more so considering the conditions in which most of us—and most of our students—are operating. It does no good to cling to an idea of hope without a clear plan to operationalize that hope for the student who needs screen-reader assistance or the group of first-years who were underserved by their high school education. This is where we are ill-served by the airy appeals to inspiration that suffuse some of the educational literature. As Henry Giroux has repeatedly insisted, critical pedagogy must speak not only the "language of critique," but the "language of possibility" or "language of hope" in order to make a real difference in the lives of both faculty and students. For Giroux, "the language of hope goes beyond how power works as a mechanism of domination and offers up a vocabulary in which it becomes possible to imagine power working in the interest of justice, equality, and freedom."[6] Once the rubber hits the road for the semester, when that first wave of assignments comes in, or the unexpected-yet-somehow-expected problems crop up, though, it's easy to get wrapped up in the language of critique and simply remain in that space. Even if we're able to recognize that and keep moving, it's also easy to speak the language of hope only vaguely and hesitantly, avoiding getting specific about difficult choices and actions that fill us with anxiety.

This is when we have to ask: *what is my next action, now?* A vision of teaching with radical hope that's grounded first and foremost in our everyday decisions and practices helps us sustain our commitment to its principles—especially when we're struggling with the seemingly endless tide of things to think about, respond to, and do on a daily basis. Creating spaces in which these principles are manifest in our practice, spaces in which all of our students have an equitable opportunity to learn, as well as be seen for the full and complicated human beings they are, provides the essential foundation for teaching with radical hope. But those spaces do not spring out of our heads into existence, fully formed; the processes through which we create them take time, work, and committed and intentional thought. Once we open these still-developing spaces to students, though, we can turn our attention to what we're doing within them even as they continue to take shape.

INTO PRACTICE

Create a list, if it doesn't exist already, of the resources available in your institution to support Universal Design for Learning. Are most of them housed in a teaching and learning center, or in the IT department, or in your office of disability services? Discover how students navigate your institution's process for seeking assistance or accommodations for their learning. If your list is decentralized, or if there is little/no support for UDL, consider the ways in which you might (if your position allows for it) advocate for greater clarity and/or resources. What would be the first step you could take in that advocacy?

Consider doing a course materials accessibility check. There are online resources that can help you assess such documents as your syllabus (Tulane University's Accessible Syllabus Project at accessiblesyllabus.com) or materials you've created and/or posted online (the W3C's Web Accessibility Initiative at https://www.w3.org/WAI/fundamentals /accessibility-intro/). Are your course materials accessible to all of your students? Are there areas where they aren't? What are the next steps you might take to make them more accessible?

CHAPTER 6

ENCOURAGING CHOICE, COLLABORATION, AND AGENCY

I didn't go to graduate school to be a cell phone cop.

This may seem like a self-evident proposition, but it certainly didn't feel that way about eight or nine years ago, when it seemed like the ubiquity of cell phones—and their technological kin, the laptop computer—posed an existential threat to education as we know it. Complaint after article after Facebook post after lamentation from educators of all stripes gave the impression that our students were so focused on texting or updating their status that learning had simply ground to a halt. What were we going to do when faced with this threat to our classroom authority? The predominant answer, at least among my colleagues and social networks, was to adopt a hard-line policy. No phones in class. Laptops shut. One instructor went so far as to have students leave their phones on a table at the front of the classroom before they sat down. My students told me of another faculty member who, when a student's phone rang in class, grabbed the offending device, strode to the front desk, and dunked it in the tall cup of water they brought with them to teach. I guess that sent a message. But I remain unsure exactly what that message was.

Yet, as a relatively new faculty member, I still felt like I needed to pick a side. Where would I make my stand—with those who wanted to keep the classroom a genuine learning space, or with those who sought to resist and undermine that goal? Of course, when the issue was presented that way, the result was predetermined. In the name of learning, I instituted a sweeping tech ban in my courses. I tried to couch it in humor, telling my students that I reserved the right to answer any phone that rang during class time, but my intent was ironclad: hide your technology, because we would be *learning* here, dammit. That ban lasted all of one day. A student who had a partner in intensive care at the hospital needed to be able to receive texts or calls, and assured me she would keep her phone on vibrate and sit near the door in case she needed to discreetly leave to take an emergency call. Was I going to say no to that request? Of course not. Then, a few days later, we were discussing a particular document and a student asked about the author's historical context. Unsure of some of the particulars, I asked if anyone could take their phone out to do a quick Google search. "I thought you banned us from using our phones," a student remarked. We all chuckled, but we were able to get our questions answered quickly, and the information ended up adding to the discussion. After that class, though, I began to wonder if my technology ban wasn't the pedagogical equivalent of machine-gunning a mosquito.

There's since been some evolution in the ways in which both faculty and students work with technology in the classroom, and my own classroom practice reflects that development. Sure, there are still calls to ban laptops, detonate cell phones, or other instances of tilting at digital windmills, but many faculty are able to navigate the issue of technology in the classroom with more nuance and awareness. What I learned when I reflected on both the reasons for and the results of my attempt at a digital embargo is that when we say we're struggling with students doing distracting things on their devices, we often mistake the symptom for the actual problem. From the times when paper and pencil replaced the slate board for student work, there have always been laments about how new technologies have somehow corrupted the learning process and destroyed students' attention spans. We've always had distracted students, whether that distraction involved staring out the window at the quad on a beautiful spring afternoon or sitting in the lecture hall's back row and updating their fantasy football lineup. (It's worth noting that the same holds true for most faculty meetings I've attended in my career.) The question we should be asking ourselves is what accounts for those distractions? Is it the mere presence of a laptop? Or is that laptop simply the closest outlet for a student who doesn't feel any connection to what's happening in the class? Sure, there are studies that show us how tempting our devices are, how that quick dopamine hit from a Twitter "like" feels so good. But lying underneath that surface behavior is the impetus for distraction in the first place.

That was the realization I came to in my own practice: if a student got distracted, well, that happens sometimes and I can work to bring them back into orbit. But if a whole bunch of my students are surfing the internet on their tablets and laptops, perhaps it's not them as much as me serving as the common denominator in this classroom problem. I could continue to try and police devices and behavior, or I could work to incorporate elements into my pedagogy that invited students not only to connect with my course but perhaps to take ownership of their learning (and the tools they used in its service) as well. In the end, it wasn't much of a choice at all: I could play the heavy (a role for which I find myself increasingly ill-suited), or I could collaborate with my students to find solutions that worked for all of us. By reflecting critically on what I was doing—and not doing—with my course policies and design, I was able to arrive at a solution that worked well for my courses, largely removing the problem of device-distracted students.

Being critically reflective about our pedagogical practice is so important because faculty possess a great degree of power, and we wield that power in significant ways whether we're aware of it or not. The choices we make (or, conversely, those we avoid making) shape the learning environment our students encounter. Being cognizant of this power, and realizing how it works on an everyday basis, helps us use it in ways that work for, rather than against, student learning. There are lots of specific ways in which we can leverage our power in this fashion, but paradoxically, we use it most effectively when we give it away. For example, if we're thinking about creating a space in which effective and meaningful teaching and learning can occur, then we should consider how that space might be best fashioned in collaboration with our students. In other words, rather than bringing students into the house after the furniture's been moved in and it's already been painted, maybe they can help us decorate and furnish the space in which we'll all live during the course. We know that student motivation increases in direct variation with the degree of control or autonomy they perceive themselves as having in a course. We also know that increased motivation has all sorts of positive effects on learning.[1] This seems like a pretty compelling case for creating room for our students to have a voice in our course design—the very creation of their learning space. This type of collaboration can build a sense of agency for students, encouraging them to take ownership of their learning, which in turn opens up a range of pedagogical strategies that we can employ to good effect throughout the course.

Collaborative Expectation Setting

One effective way we can collaborate with our students to shape the course experience is through setting expectations as a class community, rather than simply listing a set of policies on the syllabus we hand to them on the first day of class. What if the syllabus had a blank section under the header "class expectations," and we invited our students to write that section collectively? This was actually the approach I landed upon to solve the dilemma surrounding technology in my class. I asked my students to help frame the expectations for our class that semester, beginning the conversation with two questions: what helps you learn, and what gets in the way of your learning? I shared some research with them about how off-task device use not only distracts the student on their device, but others around them as well, thus framing the discussion as one about reciprocity and collegiality. It's one thing to mentally check out, but to do so in ways that essentially steal others' attention without their having a choice in the matter casts the issue in a different light. From this shared understanding, my students and I were able to collaboratively create a set of expectations we agreed to abide by over the semester.

There's a real value to this kind of exercise. Indeed, one of the best outcomes for us as instructors is we don't have to be the behavior police. The class community itself defined the expectations, so every member of that community is responsible for maintaining them. It takes the power imbalance and hierarchical nature of faculty-student dynamics out of the equation. If a student has their laptop open and is shopping on Amazon during group work, and the class has set the expectation that this time needs to be device free so everyone is fully present with their group, then I don't have to call that student out in front of their peers or play laptop cop. Instead, I only have to remind that student what we all agreed to as a class. The adversarial tone is removed, and the issue likely doesn't rise to the level of distraction. The idea of classroom management is an outmoded, stultifying concept that denies that our students play an active role in their learning. Far better to practice collective conversation and collaborative expectation setting to ensure our classrooms (whether face-to-face or online) are the type of learning spaces they need to be for engaged teaching and learning.

Setting expectations collaboratively can be particularly valuable for courses where the primary vehicle of instruction and interaction is group discussion. If you are conducting a seminar or a workshop-type course, so much depends upon students' interactions with you, the material, and one another occurring in a skillful and collegial way. Rather than simply declaring in your syllabus "students should respect one another during class discussions," consider a conversation with students about what respect means to them. Indeed, every semester when I do collaborative expectation setting and ask students what they think general course expectations should be, the most frequent response I get is some variation of "show respect." It's important, though, to dig deeper and help students conceive of respect as something more than just a vague concept. What does respect look like in a discussion in which there are vehement disagreements about perspectives or interpretations? How do we demonstrate respect for one another in a conversation about difficult, controversial, or sensitive topics? Having students consider, for example, how they would want a peer to react to something they said even if they disagreed with its premise can be a clarifying exercise for creating "rules of the road" for class discussions. It's one thing for students to agree to show respect for one another in a general sense, but it's more meaningful for them to articulate precisely how they'd like to be treated by their peers in specific conversational contexts and then consider the ways they can reciprocate (no interrupting or cross talk, for example). Collaborative expectation setting with a specific focus on the discussion environment is an excellent way to preemptively mitigate some of the issues that can derail discussions later in the semester.

Offering Students Choices

Another way to invite our students into the course-design conversation is to offer assignment choice. I want to acknowledge here that for some teaching situations, this might not be feasible, however. If you're teaching a course with standardized assignments across sections, or if you're a new and/or adjunct faculty member who might not be in a position to do this type of pedagogical tinkering, your scope of action is limited. But if the room exists to do so, it's worth thinking about allowing students to select from a range of options to complete at least the major assessments in your course. Some instructors design their courses so that students use a "choose your own adventure" model to select the various assignments and timelines they will use to fulfill the course requirements.[2] Others offer different means for students to complete a semester-long course project (research paper, digital exhibit, model curriculum unit, or oral presentation) or even something as basic as multiple prompts from which to choose in completing an essay assignment. For some faculty, student autonomy and choice are part of the grading mechanism for the course, through the use of "specifications grading," or where students can contract for specific grades.[3] The common thread running through these specific course-design techniques is their cession of a significant degree of control to students.

One of my favorite methods of assignment choice is the "unessay," a type of project I first encountered through the writings of Ryan Cordrell, an English professor at Northeastern University (though the idea originated with Daniel Paul O'Donnell at the University of Lethbridge). Cordrell tells his students that, in principle, an essay can be a powerful and creative way to articulate and express ideas. But all too often, he says, "the essay form, which should be extremely free and flexible, is instead often presented as a static and rule-bound monster that students must master in order not to lose marks . . . far from an opportunity to explore intellectual passions and interests in a personal style, the essay is transformed into a formulaic method." Enter the unessay, which is exactly what the name implies—the opposite of the stultifying formula that restricts student expression, and thus constrains the ways in which students might demonstrate their learning. As Cordrell puts it, "the unessay is an assignment that attempts to undo the damage done by this approach to teaching writing. It works by throwing out all the rules you have learned about essay writing in the course of your primary, secondary, and post secondary education and asks you to focus instead solely on your intellectual interests and passions. In an unessay you choose your own topic, present it any way you please, and are evaluated on how compelling and effective you are."[4]

While this may seem so latitudinarian as to render assessment meaningless, the unessay actually allows students to engage with the course material and produce work that is meaningful, creative, and amply demonstrates the degree of learning that's occurred. By allowing students the freedom to concentrate on creating and expressing knowledge, as opposed to fitting their work into a format they had no hand in defining, we give them the space to produce some spectacular results. Examples of unessay successes abound. One history professor who used unessays for his US history survey noted that "students in my class have used the project as an opportunity to explore those aspects of the early American past left underexplored in the textbook and only tangentially covered (if at all) in our class discussion," and submitted work such as a music major's original piano composition about slavery and freedom and a landscape management student's landscape blueprints of an indigenous American village both before and after the beginnings of English colonization.[5] Some faculty offer students the opportunity to choose between a traditional research essay project or the unessay, which only serves to bolster the element of choice that makes this type of activity so valuable for students.[6]

In addition to providing a compelling method by which students can accomplish various learning outcomes, assignment choice, as well as specific practices like the un-essay, grant students the agency to construct a meaningful narrative of their learning. Any time we can give students such opportunities to reflect not only on what they've learned, but about themselves *as learners*, we help them develop agency. When students see themselves as not just the recipients of content but as knowledge producers, as architects of their own learning, then they reap the full benefits of higher education. But in order to create the space in which they can do all of this, we have to be willing to cede much of the power we hold over our course and the way it unfolds. We have to be willing to let students experiment and create, rather than pushing everyone through the content in lock-step. For academics, giving up control can be a frightening proposition, and certainly one that runs counter to how we were trained to be the expert in our subject area. Once again, though, our pedagogical power is best used when we share it with students. Sure, we can be a content expert, and know more than anyone on campus about the subject at hand. But if we can't meaningfully teach—not recite or convey, but *teach*—that knowledge, it's rendered useless. Knowledge shouldn't be something that's set up on a shelf, to be admired but not touched or interacted with. Knowledge is meant to live in the world, to be transmitted, to help students actively intervene in their own reality.[7] Teaching from a pedagogical standpoint that sees and values students as colleagues in this mutual scholarly enterprise is the best way we can ensure that our knowledge is an active force in shaping a more just world. And in order to teach this way, we need to conceive of our courses as inclusive spaces that offer our students a meaningful role in shaping their learning.

INTO PRACTICE

What are the student habits or behaviors that have most frustrated you or your colleagues? Are there ways in which the types of collaborative work on classroom expectations discussed in this chapter might ameliorate some of these? Consider how you might alter or increase student involvement in setting policy for your courses.

Examine the high-stakes assessments (e.g., term projects, research papers) for one of your courses. Consider doing a mind map or freewrite that explores alternate forms in which students might demonstrate their fulfillment of these assignments' learning goals. Are there several roads to these outcomes, or one particular path? How might this exercise inform the assignment design and assessment plans for your courses?

CHAPTER 7

A SYLLABUS WORTH READING

Read the Syllabus!

If I had a dollar for every time I've heard that phrase (or its close cousin *It's in the [@#^$%] syllabus!*) over the entirety of my faculty career, I'd have paid off my student loans a lot sooner. *Read the syllabus* is the most common lament of higher education practitioners, isn't it? If we were to judge solely by the sheer volume of T-shirts, coffee mugs, note-pads, and other tchotchkes inscribed with this phrase that one can purchase online, the only logical conclusion would be that not a single student ever read the syllabus for any of their courses throughout their college career. All of the attention and labor that faculty put into constructing their syllabi have been wasted, as students apparently refuse to read these documents, or are unable to because they've already misplaced them. Even if they do read the syllabus, the conventional wisdom goes, they forget every important part before midterms. But this cynical trope doesn't describe the students with whom I've worked throughout my career. Sure, there are a few here and there who didn't read the syllabus, but I think when it comes to this lament about syllabus illiteracy, we are often the architects of our own frustrations. If we insist that students are to read the syllabus, have we devoted the thought and energy to creating something worth reading? As faculty, we understand the inherent importance of an effective syllabus for a successful course. But are we making that importance explicit to our students?

As the saying goes, you never get a second chance to make a first impression. If we are setting about the business of creating learning spaces that are inclusive and accessible, which embody a pedagogy centered in radical hope, we need to remain mindful of the first impressions of those spaces our students will receive. As more and more of our institutions utilize online platforms or learning management systems, and as an increasing amount of our teaching happens in a blended or fully online format, a posted syllabus is increasingly likely to be the initial contact our students have with either us or the course. Even if that's not the case, the syllabus certainly plays a significant role at the beginning of a course, and should both align with and accurately reflect the pedagogical principles we want to enact. While most, if not all, of our institutions have policies, checklists, or even templates for course syllabi, and we are told ad nauseam that the syllabus is the equivalent of a legal contract, I want to issue a challenge that we think about the document beyond these purely instrumental, transactional terms. In this chapter, my purpose is not to relitigate the specific things that should or should not appear in a course syllabus (though I have some thoughts about certain essential elements) or provide some sort of critical syllabus checklist. Rather, I want to suggest ways to reconceive the syllabus as the crucial first step in enacting a meaningful pedagogical approach to the teaching and learning with which we and our students will engage. In doing so, I would argue that we can create a powerful and dynamic map for our course that will not just inform, but empower our students.

The Promises We Make

If we've been mindful and persistent about our pedagogical approach as manifested in the concrete decisions about the learning spaces we're creating, then the syllabus—again, what might well be our students' first formal encounter with those spaces—looms large. If the syllabus is indeed the initial encounter, or at least close to it, between us and our students, we should be mindful of the ways it can shape that encounter for both good and ill. If we create syllabi that are simply information dumps or policy sheets, it's hard for us to stand before our students and talk about things like active learning, engagement, and collaboration. If there's more space devoted to the consequences of violating some norm than there is to how we can help students succeed in the course, is that something that aligns with our larger pedagogical approach? If we want our students to actively engage as learners, and to take some ownership of that process, can we present them with a syllabus full of distant, impersonal boilerplate language that holds them at a distance rather than inviting them in? The syllabus represents one important opportunity for us to connect with our students in ways that are inviting and authentic, but all too often, it's an opportunity many of us don't take full advantage of.

In his book *What the Best College Teachers Do*, Ken Bain describes an approach he calls the "promising syllabus." Reviewing the syllabi of a wide range of effective college teachers, Bain identified several characteristics they held in common, even across a wide range of disciplines and pedagogies. The common denominator of promising syllabi is that each "fundamentally recognizes that people will learn best and most deeply when they have a strong sense of control over their own education rather than feeling manipulated by someone else's demands."[1] Promising syllabi place students at the center of the learning environment they describe; the emphasis is not on what the course will cover so much as what students will take with them from the course. They also "begin a conversation" (as opposed to an instructor's monologue) about how students will know what they're learning and how effectively they're doing so. And finally, this type of syllabus makes clear to students what they will be asked to do to see the promises of the course fulfilled for them. The promising syllabus has student learning, not instructors or institutions, firmly at its center. This is a subtle, seemingly simple shift, but one that has extraordinary consequences.

I think we ought to extend Bain's concept to embrace the fact that *all* syllabi are "promising": implicitly or explicitly, they are making promises to our students, whether we realize it or not. So what are we promising them? A syllabus that contains page after page of policy-and-consequence speech, lengthy descriptions of what constitutes plagiarism and what the punishments for it are, promises students that you will see them as trying to game the system until proven otherwise. Syllabi with language like "the instructor will . . ." and "the learner/student must . . ." promise students a sterile, impersonal course experience. Syllabi with no course calendar or explanation of assignments and criteria make a promise to students that assessment will be arbitrary, and likely frustrating. A syllabus that's proscriptive—more *thou shalt not* than anything else—promises a course with a wide gulf between students and the instructor, where empathy or compassion will be in short supply. We may not intend for those promises to be made, but the syllabi that at least initially serve as our surrogates make them nonetheless.

How do we avoid making the wrong promises to our students? One of the most important considerations is to ensure that what we say and how we say it are in alignment: does our syllabus make the same promises to our students we would make to them in person? It's easy to lose track of how important style and tone are for a course syllabus, especially when we're being asked to include an increasing amount of disclaimers and institutional policy statements in the document, or when there's a mile-long checklist— complete with arcane terminology—of things we absolutely *must* include lest the deans swoop down upon us with fell vengeance. Even within various constraints, though, I would argue there's room for us to shift style and tone in a positive direction. One strategy is to personalize our language; "I" and "you" (or even "y'all" if that's your thing) create a better sense of immediacy and rapport than the third-person objective tense. Personal pronouns also make it easier for us to emphasize the type of promises we want to make: "as a result of this course, you will be able to do the following . . ." is a good way to introduce your course goals, for example, as it centers the student's experience and renders the outcomes tangible for them.

Speaking of course goals, I suggest they occupy pride of place at or near the beginning of the syllabus. These are the promises, in the sense Bain uses the term; the course goals should express what students will be able to do that they couldn't before (or do better than they could before) as a result of participating in your course—but how so, exactly? Answering that question will help you frame goals not only around specific course content, but embracing the larger intellectual or metacognitive skills that students will be able to develop. We all believe our disciplines are important not just because of specific knowledge they contribute, but also the modes of analysis or habits of mind that they inculcate. I don't teach very many history majors at all in my 100-level surveys, but my course goals include elements of "thinking like a historian" that are of larger importance. I make the case to my students that doing historical research and analysis will help them develop tools like critical information literacy and the ability to meaningfully understand different perspectives—tools that will serve them well no matter where their academic journey leads them. In other words, I'm making certain promises about how the course will be a valuable and significant learning experience for them, no matter what their major might be.

Reframing Policy Language

We can also ensure that we're making the right kind of promises to our students by blunting the sharp edges of policy statements and presenting them in ways that don't make it appear that we think it's not *if*, but *when*, students will do something wrong. My institution, for example, has a rather lengthy policy on academic integrity. It not only discusses what constitutes academic dishonesty, but lays out the specific steps of the process whereby students are notified of a violation, how they can appeal that decision, and also what happens as a result of a second or third offense. All of these elements are important, but including the whole discussion in the course syllabus means that I'd be devoting nearly two full pages to a deep dive on what's essentially a crime-and-punishment discussion. Including our statement of academic integrity (a brief paragraph), referring to where students can find the complete policy statement if they're interested, and then providing a brief explanation of why I believe academic honesty is an important component of responsible and ethical scholarship is a much better way to address the issue. It's less adversarial, and grounds the issue not in a punitive discourse but rather a positively framed ethical expectation for all of us as we build our collective scholarly endeavor.

That's one example of how we might reposition the various policy matters we might be obligated to include in our syllabus. Another technique to consider is adding personalized language to otherwise institutional-sounding disclosures. For example, most institutions have language to use for students with disabilities regarding requests for accommodation and other services. This language, however, is usually impersonal and bureaucratic, instructing "the student" to consult "the disabilities services office for the necessary forms" to present to "the instructor." For students who might already be anxious and unsure about the process of asking for (perfectly legitimate and necessary) assistance with their learning, perhaps we might reframe this section in more personal and inviting terms. There's no reason the typical disabilities-accommodations section of a course syllabus couldn't be expanded into a statement of our philosophy regarding student learning in general. What if, instead of the typical fare of institutional office-speak, we wrote something like what Davidson College's Mark Sample uses:

> I am committed to the principle of universal learning. This means that our classroom, our virtual spaces, our practices, and our interactions be as inclusive as possible. Mutual respect, civility, and the ability to listen and observe others carefully are crucial to universal learning. Any student with particular needs should contact [Name], the Academic Access and Disability Resources Coordinator, at the start of the semester. The Dean of Students' office will forward any necessary information to me. Then you and I can work out the details of any accommodations needed for this course.

While this statement does the same policy-oriented work as a typical disability and accommodations clause, and occupies basically the same amount of space, it foregrounds the message that learning occurs in diverse ways.[2] The accommodations part doesn't come until the second half of the paragraph; the main emphasis is on an inclusive approach to learning for *all* students. A modification like this one is a perfect example of what James M. Lang has called "small teaching," which is "an approach that seeks to spark positive change in higher education through small but powerful changes to our course design and teaching practices." The initial investment of time is so small as to be mundane (as opposed to overhauling or redesigning significant portions of our courses), but the payoff is significant.[3] This type of language change not only sets a more inclusive tone for our course, but conveys to our students that we've made specific choices about the course we've created—choices reflecting a philosophy firmly grounded in making learning accessible for *all*, and not just certain subsets of, our students.

Here I Stand

Moreover, I would argue that we should pay far more attention than is usually the case to our philosophy—the principles and ideals that underlay our pedagogy—in our syllabi and other front-facing materials. These materials are a powerful opportunity to speak to both our students and other external audiences about why what we're doing is so essential. If we're going to advocate for a higher educational system that is equitable, inclusive, and an undeniable social good, then we should think about how we present our courses—the most visible expression of our pedagogy—to those with whom we wish to advocate. I recognize that, for many of us, the most familiar incarnation of the teaching philosophy statement is the one that often goes into the application materials for an academic position. What I have in mind, though, is a brief and accessible distillation of our principles designed for immediate impact and consumption; think of the relationship between the "elevator talk" and an entire thesis or dissertation, and you'll get what I'm envisioning here. At the forefront of the syllabus, we offer a lot of information about our various locations—where our office is, where we are virtually via email or phone, and the like. We should also provide perhaps the most important piece of information about locations here: where we stand with our pedagogy.

Try this for a thought exercise: If your students were asked to describe you as a teacher in one word, what would they say? What would you hope they decide to say? And do the answers to each of these questions align? Obviously, one's entire pedagogy can't be fully conveyed in merely one word. But there are words we would be happy to have represent our philosophy (*enthusiastic, caring, interesting*), and also those we hope don't attach to our teaching (*boring, mean, condescending*). Thinking about an abbreviated description of our pedagogy can help frame the type of statement that effectively conveys, via its inclusion in your syllabus, your teaching philosophy to your students. Other questions you might consider include:

Why do you teach? Is it the passion for your discipline? The chance to try and answer the big questions? The opportunity to see students grow in their learning, make connections, achieve intellectual awakening? Articulate what it is, specifically, that energizes you about teaching.

Why do you teach this class in particular? Do you particularly enjoy teaching introductory or survey-level classes? If so, why? For an upper-level class, is it the seminar experience that attracts you? The chance to do advanced research/lab procedures/fieldwork/theoretical discussions? Even if this is a course we're teaching only because our turn came up in the rotation, or no one else in the department wanted to, there's still *something* we can say, even if it's along the lines of "this course gives me a chance to teach outside my principal area of research, and I'm looking forward to exploring this subject with you."

How do you think learning occurs best? Do you think students need to actively participate in order for the course to be meaningful? Are you using a pedagogy (such as flipped learning or team-based learning) different from what students typically encounter? If so, why do you use this method, and how is it the better alternative for your students? Think about what things you know make students successful, and how you can endorse them.

What does "success" mean? How will students know they've succeeded in this course? Is it defined by how much content they remember, skills in which they've gained proficiency, or something else? Or a blend of all of these? What will they take with them from this course that will be of benefit to them in the future? Students will be different as a result of having taken your course; they should be able to identify both how and why that's the case.

Many of our disciplinary fields place a premium on a sense of scholarly detachment, or even an avowed "objectivity." If you've been trained in one of them, perhaps you struggle with explicitly avowing what look to be subjective and affective, rather than objective, methods. The injection of personal ethics into what we typically treat as a scholarly milieu might feel inappropriate; some would argue it's unbecoming and unprofessional of faculty to do so. I disagree. As teachers and scholars, we take stances all the time. We're quantitative researchers; we're committed to the Socratic method; we're behaviorists; we're neo-Kantians—those are stances. So too are the choices we *don't* make, or at least aren't conscious of. Defaulting to solely sage-on-the-stage lecturing is a stance. Not teaching the survey course unless we *really* have to is a stance. As the Rush song goes, "if you choose not to decide, you still have made a choice."[4] Embracing our teaching philosophy and making it transparent to our students is taking a stance, sure, but it's one we know will have positive outcomes. It humanizes us (and, by extension, our course and its material) in the eyes of our students. It invites our students to be collaborators in learning, as opposed to merely recipients of knowledge. It promises that our course has not only content- or discipline-specific value to them, but will also make a difference in significant ways no matter what academic path they subsequently take. And, not least of all, it commits us to a practice that is in alignment with our principles and commitment to our vision of what higher education ought to embody. All of these elements make for a compelling learning experience, one students can feel connected to and empowered by.

There's no law stating that the course syllabus must be an antiseptic collection of policy statements, or a terse list of what not to do in the course; the force of academic custom merely makes it appear as if that's the case. Think back to your own undergraduate experience: perhaps you had a course where, once you saw the syllabus, you were intrigued and—dare I say?—excited. If you didn't have that experience, think of the difference it would have made. A fancy syllabus isn't a substitute for effective pedagogy, and promising language isn't self-fulfilling. But if we're committed to a pedagogy standing on radical hope in who our students are, and what we and our institutions can help them become, then we ought to demonstrate that commitment whenever opportunities avail themselves. The course syllabus is one such opportunity, and an important one at that. Approaching our syllabi as the crucial first impression of our course, as a way to invite students to become collaborators in a significant learning experience, is an easy change to make. Being thoughtful about what we're communicating to our students in this document, and being intentional about how we're doing so, moves the syllabus from simply representing a transaction to embodying a real transformation. If learning is to be transformational, then let's ensure that the ways in which we create the spaces for it to occur embody that spirit.

INTO PRACTICE

What do your syllabi look like from a student perspective? Consider having a colleague from well outside your discipline read your syllabus and offer feedback on its clarity, organization, and content. A resource that might assist with this activity is the "Syllabus from a Student Perspective" checklist, which may be accessed online at http:// www.thetattooedprof.com/wp-content/uploads/2019/09 /The-Syllabus-from-a-student-perspective.pdf.

Make a word cloud from your syllabus, using one of the several free online word cloud generators (like wordclouds.com, for example). Using this visual representation of your syllabus text (and disregarding results like "the" and "of"), what words appear most frequently? Does this pattern align with the type of tone and approach you want your syllabus to have? What revisions, elisions, or additions might you make to your syllabi to make them more inclusive and effective?

—

CHAPTER 8

PEDAGOGY IS NOT A WEAPON

—

Ever since Socrates spent long Athenian afternoons upbraiding his followers in the Agora, there has been a venerable tradition among educators to complain about our students or their various foibles. We all do it, and there's no denying that this type of venting can serve a valuable purpose, if kept to the private and confidential realm of office talks or water-cooler chatter with colleagues. But student shaming has moved beyond the confines of faculty-lounge venting and become a cottage industry of sorts, as the past few years have shown that it can pay to be an educator with pissed-off hot takes about Kids These Days™.

I don't mean to say there isn't room for critiques of how students interact with higher education (and vice versa). But I do find it odd that, in bestselling books by "thought leaders" or the op-ed pages of the *New York Times* or the *Atlantic*, this genre chooses to blame students for being victimized by the very structural problems the authors lament. Calling students "the dumbest generation" and justifying that claim by pointing to their consumption of digital media and use of digital tools begs the question: what exactly are students supposed to do? Opt out of the internet? Describing Ivy League students as "excellent sheep"—strong academic performers but safely orthodox thinkers—doesn't really address the larger question of why students might be intellectually conditioned to be that way (and whose interests such conditioning might serve). One might ask, is the Ivy League's culture one where that sort of sheep-ness is the implicit norm, an attitude through which students see the easiest path to success (almost always defined as a degree)?[1] If we bemoan that equation of success with degree attainment and complain that students only see higher education in terms of what type of job they will get, have we paused to realize that this is what students have been told by teachers, parents, and politicians from their very first discussions of college? *Go to college to get a better job. A bachelor's degree increases your future earning power.* How do admissions counselors recruit students (and parents/extended families)? By using things like job placement rates of our recent graduates. Even in the liberal arts, we defend the value of our disciplines largely by talking about how a liberal arts education imparts the types of skills employers value. *You'll be a capitalist cog, but a thoughtful one!* So how can we fault students for seeing higher education in largely instrumental, transactional terms if those are the only terms in which they've had it presented to them? We cannot blame students for the failures of the systems in which we've forced them to operate. If we want to restore the idea of higher education as a space of transformation, of emancipatory learning, then we need to start with the ways in which we talk about its purpose and value. Have we adopted the language of instrumental reason and neoliberal ideology to justify our worth? If so, any victory won with these measures will be fleeting at best, and any space we create for ourselves will contract even more suddenly than it appeared.

Understanding Safe Spaces and Trigger Warnings

One of the most damaging ways in which neoliberal ideology and values have infected our current higher education discourse is manifest in the outrage ginned up by conservative academics and organizations over so-called trigger warnings and safe spaces. Like many topics that have become fodder for this anger-industrial complex, trigger warnings and safe spaces exist in this debate only as thin caricatures, targets du jour for those who embrace an anti-student and anti-learning agenda. A particularly egregious example comes from within the academy itself, a now famous (or notorious) 2016 letter from the University of Chicago's dean of students to the university's incoming class of new students.[2] Less of a welcome letter than a polemic searching for an audience, the dean's letter cautioned the new students that no matter what they might have heard, higher education is No Place for Timid Men. Contrary to the prevailing trends in higher education, the dean averred, the University of Chicago was not in the business of shielding students from arguments they didn't like. *No, Sir, this august institution was not in the business of creating "safe spaces"; sometimes the truth hurts, sometimes you have to hear arguments you don't like, and sometimes life is just hard, dammit.* The dean's implication was clear: the university is here to toughen students up, not serve as a nanny bent on tucking its students away, comfortably shielded from scary ideas and the big, bad world. The letter went viral almost instantly, and judging by the number of approving shares and "YAAASS" endorsements it received on various social media platforms, the dean clearly touched a nerve. In an impressive yet ultimately dismaying feat of irony, the defenders of Chicago's tough-love approach shouted down anyone who disagreed with them, mocking and denigrating the dean's critics as a bunch of safe-space-wanting hippies not worthy of being involved in the conversation. Never mind that a large proportion of these critics were actual teachers who had actual experience with actual students; the narrative of a stern father figure telling the trophy generation to buck up was too compelling to resist.

These types of arguments, though, take aim at a caricature rather than reality. The backlash against so-called safe spaces fundamentally misunderstands the concept. The critics of trigger warnings fall into the same trap; they concentrate their fire on a bogeyman that exists mostly in their own fevered imaginations. Those of us who employ these pedagogical tools understand that creating a safe space for discussion isn't a means to hide from scary topics, but rather to ensure that all participants can engage and struggle with them on equitable terms. It heightens the quality of analysis, and significantly adds to the degree of learning that takes place, if students know that they will be treated with respect and collegiality while wrestling with difficult, emotional, or sensitive topics. John Palfrey argues we might use the term "brave spaces" to define these environments. Students ought to bravely confront ideas with which they disagree or that pose the risk of discomfort. But, Palfrey continues, teachers and institutions need to do a much better job providing the structure and support necessary for these spaces to work, as well as the structure to keep these spaces functioning as genuine areas of dialogue rather than the rhetorical equivalent of a Hobbesian state of nature.[3] Safe spaces—the real version, not the trumped-up caricature—do not hide ideas from students, but rather create an environment in which those ideas can actually receive the engagement and scrutiny they merit.

So too with trigger warnings (which, given the nature of the conversation surrounding them, might more constructively be called "content warnings"). These are pedagogical tools that allow for genuine engagement and confrontation with ideas and material, and in fact are the only tools that allow us to do so. You cannot have a discussion about difficult material that includes all students if some of those students are sitting in shocked silence and others are devoting cognitive resources to maintaining an outward equilibrium or suppressing an anxiety attack. You cannot honestly confront difficult material if there are students unprepared to participate in that process, and our students will certainly need varying degrees of preparation. You may think you're being clever by utilizing shock value as a teaching tool, but more likely you're just being an asshole. Somewhere along the way, the idea that it might be a good thing to warn students if they would be encountering, say, unusually racist or violent material has morphed into an assault on the very bastions of academic freedom. *Why should we give students an out? Won't they just use it as an escape hatch to avoid any and all course work they "don't like"?* But, once again, that's not how any of this works. We live with trigger warnings all around us, for what else are movie ratings or the "viewer discretion advised" disclaimers at the beginning of a television show if not a similar mechanism?

To use a more direct classroom example: we know that a significant portion of women (perhaps 1 in 4) are sexually harassed or assaulted in college. Extrapolating from those numbers (which are underreported, if anything), there's a better than average chance that one of my students is a survivor of sexual assault. And let's say I show a portion of the film *Twelve Years a Slave* in one of my class sessions, a portion that includes the scene in which a white overseer rapes an enslaved woman. Now imagine being a student who has been sexually assaulted, who is perhaps still working with a counselor, and who has experienced PTSD-like symptoms from the attack—and without warning, you're watching a violent rape unfold on the screen in front of you as a part of class. What are your options? You can leave the room, but draw unwanted attention to yourself and perhaps fuel rumors and gossip. Or you can remain and relive your nightmare, complete with the physical symptoms of post-traumatic stress, in the middle of the classroom. If only you'd known what was going to happen beforehand, you could have either not watched that scene, left the room beforehand, or availed yourself of one of a number of other options, perhaps in consultation with the professor.

To shift back to the faculty perspective: knowing what I know about the likelihood of a scene triggering some sort of trauma in a student's experience, why would I not do something—a brief warning or content note—to prepare the class for what was to come? This is especially true if discussion or meaningful engagement with the material is my goal; it serves no pedagogical purpose to surprise my students with potentially traumatic content. Blindsiding students with graphic material isn't teaching; it's assault. I do not believe in teaching through hazing, and I refuse to employ pedagogy as a weapon.

It is literally this simple: trigger warnings are exactly what the label says. If a student might be triggered (in the psychological trauma sense, not in the grossly oversimplified ways in which that term has been deployed by internet trolls and their ilk), a simple heads-up helps them take the necessary steps—whatever those might be—to prepare. A literature professor assigning Thomas Hardy's *Tess of the D'Urbervilles* does no harm by warning the class that rape is a key plot point, and likely helps students who might have needed such a warning to constructively engage with the novel.

You might have noticed my examples surrounding trigger warnings and the larger issue of students and trauma are centered on issues of sexual harassment and/or violence. This is by design, done to highlight one of the inescapable realities of working with students in today's college or university environment. The appallingly high numbers of sexual assaults on college campuses, coupled with the equally appalling problems that institutions of higher education have exhibited in addressing this crisis, means that it's not a matter of if, but when, we will have students in our classrooms who are dealing with this type of trauma. Moreover, there is a wider range of incidents that can prompt subsequent manifestation of trauma. Refugees, for example, have often experienced horrific circumstances in whatever journeys they took to land in our classrooms. Even more prevalently, there is the "classic" diagnosis of PTSD that stems from combat experience. As our student body continues to diversify—in areas like gender identity, ethnicity, immigration or veteran status, for example—the traumas embedded in some of our students' experiences are part of the package. It's worth observing, though, that we never see conservative commentators making fun of the things we do to mitigate the effects of combat-induced PTSD on our campuses. Yet those measures are justified by, and function in, the exact same ways as the types of trigger warnings we would use around sexual violence. That lack of criticism is revealing, and it says a lot about the conservatives' opinions regarding gender and sexual assault. It should trouble us that one of the most visible (and eminently reasonable) ways we use to demonstrate empathy and compassion for a not-insignificant number of our students has been twisted into a weapon and thrown back at us by culture warriors who seem bent upon measuring learning by the amount of suffering involved. In the process, the very phrase "trigger warning" has been turned into a punch line, its original meaning and utility so badly distorted that I hesitated to use it, even in this context. When compassion for students has become the object of derision in so many quarters, we should ask ourselves what went wrong.

Allies, Not Adversaries

These hot-take contests over content warnings and safe spaces, however, occupy only one part of the student-shaming spectrum. The higher education trope that sees students as adversaries until proven otherwise, that equates rigor with hazing, can suffuse almost every aspect of our practice if we aren't careful. Indeed, it often does—and it comes to do so early. How many of us, in our graduate student years, were socialized into assuming an affect of disdain for undergrads as a de rigueur part of our program's culture (as I discussed in chapter 3)? And it's not just cranky grad students. Surely we've all seen the ubiquitous social media posts that compile student gaffes, or rain scorn on their unskillful moments on tasks ranging from emails to essay exams. It may feel good at the time to laugh at students' foibles; when we feel like we're being squeezed by administration, or if the contract for next semester hasn't materialized yet, it can be tempting to vent our own frustrations on the students with whom, after all, we spend the most time in a job environment that can make us anxious and angry. Even if it's not the students' fault that austerity politics have eviscerated our institution's budgets, and even though they too suffer from the increasing adjunctification of the faculty, they often become the target of our antipathy simply by virtue of being present with us on a day-to-day basis. It's all too easy to have legitimate anger against unjust and inequitable institutional conditions redirected to those who deserve it the least, simply because they're the available target and because it's so easy to commiserate with peers in a common derision of others. Just as the industrialists of the late nineteenth and early twentieth centuries kept workers divided by actively stoking racial and ethnic tensions, so too do we see faculty and students often pitted against one another rather than making common cause against the dangers facing us both. As long as we're writing Facebook posts with titles like "you won't *believe* what my students wrote on this exam" or anonymous message board posts castigating students for all sorts of perceived slights, we'll do further damage to higher education because we'll be unloading on precisely the people with whom we ought to be making common cause.[4]

One doesn't have to be this overtly venomous to students in order to communicate a low regard for them. There are many ways in which we communicate disrespect for our students, often implicitly and perhaps unintentionally. For example, we tell them they're expected to act like adults but some of us require them to submit documentary evidence they were at the doctor's office or a funeral if they miss one of our classes. *Sorry about your aunt, but I need to see a copy of the funeral program in order to believe you've suffered this loss.* As discussed in chapter 7, when we load our syllabi with a page of "thou shalt not"-conduct policy strictures, or several paragraphs vividly describing the consequences for a litany of specific cheating scenarios, we're telling students we're expecting them to do something wrong, that we expect them to pounce on any opportunity to game the system, that we see them as adversaries.

This feels personal to me, because I was one of those undergraduate students who would easily have been all over the "Dear Student" message boards and roasted in a series of angry Facebook rants, if my own professors had had that route available to them and chosen it. I was, at best, an indifferent student for the first three years of my undergraduate career. I did fairly well in the classes I was interested in, and skipped the others. Poor decision after poor decision got me kicked out of the honors program before the end of my freshman year and ensured a thoroughly mediocre academic record by the time I was a junior. After a series of particularly unfortunate events led to some serious self-reflection, I finally got serious about my studies. I had professors in my major who not only supported me as I got back on track, but actively worked to help me prepare for admission to graduate school—a laughable goal at first, but one I eventually attained with their help. There is absolutely no doubt in my mind that I would not be in the position I am today without those faculty mentors who believed I could do graduate work, and encouraged me even when the task of turning around my academic career seemed overwhelming. But what if they hadn't done so? I mean, I hadn't exactly provided much evidence that I could sustain an academic turnaround, or that I would be worth the investment of time and effort. These professors could very easily have looked at my actions up to that point and drawn the eminently reasonable conclusion that I wasn't going to be able to pull it off. I'm sure I wasn't the only student they had who made poor choices or did aggravating things in their courses. They didn't *have* to do anything, but they did anyway. And now I'm a tenured full professor because of the course they helped me set.

I think about this when I'm confronted with poor decisions and aggravating behaviors from my own students in my own courses. As cathartic as it might feel to rant on social media, for example, what if the student I was subtweeting saw my words? What would I have just told them? I picture one of the professors from the years of my own undergraduate foibles going on Twitter and posting something like "Y'all—one of my students just came to class *drunk*. It's Thursday *morning*." Or "This kid says he wants to go to grad school but he can't even make it to our seminar more than once a week. GTFOH." Or "My advisee is trying to turn his grades around, but I don't know . . . he talks a good game for the amount of damage he's done." If I had seen something like that, I would have been mortified and likely just given up, even though the situation I was in was my own fault. See, I knew that—I didn't need anyone to remind me. So do my students need further hectoring about what's already done, or to be brought into a constructive dialogue about how we can try and undo the damage and move forward? Even though there are times when I'm teeth-grindingly annoyed at one of my students, I have to tell myself there were plenty of folks annoyed with me back in the day. This perspective helps keep me in a place of allyship with students, as opposed to defaulting to an adversarial mindset. Students, like us, are humans and as such, will likely mess up or make poor decisions from time to time—as we ourselves have also done. Approaching these situations from a position of common humanity rather than as a rigorous taskmaster harping on deficits offers a better chance of fixing whatever's gone awry.

It's easy to unthinkingly assume an adversarial stance toward students simply because they're a target of convenience; I see more students on a daily basis than I do faculty colleagues or administrators, so they are the ones in a position to apprehend my mood and demeanor most often. But we must remain mindful that they occupy the same frustrating structures we do in higher education. Lower institutional funding and precarious faculty employment hurts them, too. Harassment, misogyny, elitism, and other features of academe can at least indirectly rebound onto them. An adversarial attitude on the part of faculty towards students-as-category is so harmful because of the damage our *authority* wreaks when we adopt it. Within the landscape of higher education, faculty/teachers have authority—in interactions with students, this authority is essentially an a priori feature, at least as those interactions begin. In our institutions, we may not have the authority we'd like in some areas, but we do carry authority granted by both our credentials and positions as mediators of education. Henry Giroux points out that authority is not automatically oppressive, but "rather it [can be] used to intervene and shape the space of teaching and learning so as to provide students with the means for challenging society's commonsense assumptions and for analyzing the interface between their own everyday lives and those broader social formations that bear down on them." Our authority does not have to be wielded like a hammer; indeed, meaningful teaching and learning for our students means that we are mindful about how we use our authority "reflexively," to create learning spaces that "encourage dialogue, deliberation, and the power of students to raise questions."[5] So how are we using our authority? What are the spaces we're shaping with it, and where do our students fit in those spaces? These are essential questions not only for those of us in the classroom, but—as the next chapter will discuss—for our institutions as well. To what ends are we directing the authority we possess?

INTO PRACTICE

Consider the various places we encounter trigger/content warnings: "the following program contains scenes unsuitable for children" or "this story contains images of violence" in our media, for example. In what ways might these instances inform your own practice when it comes to content warnings for your courses? Consider a journal entry or freewrite that addresses the arguments for and against these practices in courses offered by your department or unit; what case is to be made, and what counterarguments can you anticipate? How might you use these insights in conversations around what is, for some, a fraught topic?

Look back on your own academic career (especially from high school forward). What were the inflection points where interactions (positive or negative) with faculty played a decisive role in shaping subsequent events? What might your own experiences offer in the way of shaping your perspective on working with your own students?

CHAPTER 9

PLATFORMS AND POWER

Imagine, if you will, this scene: *The university's annual sympo-sium has begun, an event that promises to advance the mission of the institution by tackling subjects of depth and complexity in the human condition. This year's theme is "Remembering the Shoah: Saying 'Never Again' to Genocide," challenging students and the university community to confront some of the darkest chapters of modern human history. And now, striding to the podium to deliver the keynote address, comes . . . David Irving.*

To be sure, Irving's presence was vehemently protested by nu-merous campus and community organizations, including Hillel and the Anti-Defamation League, but the administration is on record that students should be challenged by opinions "outside their comfort zone." To those students who protested the fact that a conference on the Holocaust was being keynoted by the most notorious Holocaust-denier in the Western world, the local news-paper's editorial board scoffed at their need for a so-called safe space. "The real world doesn't always conform to your precious beliefs," the newspaper editorialized, "You'd best learn that now." One of the university's professors defended the choice of Irving as a keynote speaker, declaring, "nothing is more sacred than the right of free and unfettered academic discourse in the university. In this marketplace of ideas, bad ideas will naturally be subsumed by good ones—that's how education works."

Well, it's a good thing something like this would never happen! I mean, really—the spectacle of Jewish students being lectured that Holocaust-deniers were entitled to academic platforms, and that they had to sit and take it in the name of free and open discourse? That's just beyond the pale.

Right?

You've likely guessed where I'm going with this analogy. Classroom and campus spaces throughout higher education have become sites where the purported dialogue about free speech has played out in (warning: unprofessional language ahead) increasingly fucked-up ways. I don't use that term frivolously; I'm unsure if another adjective or short phrase adequately conveys the several ways in which the discourse surrounding free speech is absolutely and absurdly broken. Most problematically, those who purport to advocate for a "marketplace of ideas" without prior constraints or internal censorship are often hurting student learning, whether by design or as the consequence of their positions carried to the logical conclusion. No one would seriously consider David Irving to be a voice that needs to be at the table when we talk about the Holocaust. His very denial of what we know to be historically and empirically true is also a denial of the very humanity of Jewish people. Yet, if we examine the cases that have attracted the most media focus on college-campus speech controversies, we find they swirl around similar figures: avowed white nationalists, peddlers of discredited

racist pseudoscience and "race realism," or advocates of immigration policies that resemble ethnic cleansing. When
does free speech become the cover by which we give official
and educational legitimacy to ideas that and speakers who
are *literally arguing* (and they are very clear about this) that
a significant number of our students are not fully human?
In a perfect world, our institutions would not deploy their
intellectual capital in the service of ideas that are both
loathsome and just plain *wrong*. But in our imperfect, messy
world, where power imbalances suffuse the very structures
of higher education in which we and our students operate,
this has become somewhat par for the course. Indeed, an emphasis on decorum—even docility—rather than honest and
rigorously critical discussion suffuses much of the outrage
over the supposed "free speech crisis" in the same way it did
for the twin bogeymen of safe spaces and trigger warnings.
We should be aware, though, who is being asked to show
decorum and respect, and precisely who is doing that asking.

Let me be very clear: I am not advocating for censorship.
I am not advocating for thought police or purges. I *am* advocating for students in particular, and higher education in
general, when I suggest that we pay much more attention
to how we are using our educational spaces to implicitly endorse or reject ideas *as educators and as institutions of higher
learning*. To use the terms of my introductory example, David
Irving has the right to say whatever he wants whenever he
wants. But he doesn't have a natural right to, nor is higher
education obligated to provide him, an official (and/or
compensated) platform to say it. This is an easy example,
though; there's not going to be a bevy of discourse-ready
academics lining up to dispute the distinction I've laid out
here. But the cases that have so exercised the present-day
free speech warriors in the op-ed pages seem murkier. From

the contretemps over the author Charles Murray's visit to Middlebury College, to chastising students at places like the University of California, Berkeley, over their rude treatment of white nationalist and self-proclaimed provocateur Milo Yiannopoulos, much of what's been called a "crisis of free speech on campus" appears to be about notions of authority and etiquette more than anything else.[1] Students are excoriated for not showing the proper deference to the eminent figures there to "exchange ideas" (as if an exchange, as opposed to an imposition, is what's really occurring), for being rude, for "shutting down" discourse. Missing from this litany about Students These Days is any serious examination of their perspective, of how students might be pushing back against our efforts to further marginalize them.

It's Not about Politeness. It's about Power.

In important ways, the idea of free speech is being weaponized against students by self-appointed gatekeepers of lofty ideals, many of whom do not themselves regularly teach students. There's nothing wrong with wanting to create a climate in which honest, meaningful, and even difficult discussions can safely occur. That climate ceases to be safe, however, when one participant casts doubt on the agency, legitimacy, or humanity of another. When that happens, the environment also ceases to be pedagogically effective: at that point, not all of our students will have equal access or opportunity to learn. Our institutions must possess a climate conducive to each and every student's opportunity to learn and to exercise full agency in doing so. This holds true for any collective learning space in our campus environments: lectures, events, ceremonies, campus discourse, and the actions of faculty and staff.

As we saw in the previous chapter with the frenzied, bad-faith criticisms of trigger warnings and safe spaces, the argument that today's students are somehow less capable of dealing with controversial ideas or being intellectually challenged is fundamentally disingenuous.[2] It reflects the impulse of the powerful to silence the powerless. It's the argument of those who see themselves as the gatekeepers of higher education and public discourse, and who see diversity as a threat, not an opportunity. These superficial characterizations make for effective sound bites and op-ed headlines, but they crumble under the weight of actual evidence. Far from being a generation of entitled snowflakes, today's college students are under siege. They have less funding, less support, learn in more dysfunctional institutions, and live in an environment that is more fractured and polarized than ever. They work more hours at more jobs than any previous generation of students, deal with more issues related to anxiety and mental health than any of their forebears, and face a postgraduate economic landscape so bleak that the Baby Boom generation is in full-on denial of its very existence. All this, and they are mocked, by generations that had it twice as good, about how it's all their fault.

One would assume that recognizing people's essential humanity is not a debate-club thought exercise, that basic civil rights should not be a question open to multiple interpretations. In prior generations, however, when higher education as a whole was overwhelmingly white and male, those assumptions did not often come into play. Faculty with endowed professorships could offer biologically deterministic arguments about a hierarchy of racial types, or make claims allegedly grounded in analytic psychology that women's capacity for scientific reasoning was inherently inferior to that of men.[3] For years, these types of claims went unchallenged, and as a result became part of the intellectual water in which academics were swimming—powerful and pervasive, yet less and less acknowledged over time. In the last several decades, however, the academy has seen significant diversification in its faculty, staff, administration, and—especially—the student body. That process of diversification has been contested and remains incomplete, but has progressed enough to create a space in which much of higher education's received wisdom and hidden curriculum have come under increased scrutiny. Groups that have traditionally held sway over the discourse, and indeed much of the very agenda, of higher education are seeing that hegemony challenged, even rejected, by larger numbers of students and faculty who do not accept an environment that conceives of them as less-than. Curricula centering the white European male experience over all others no longer float along unquestioned, but for those who have never thought to interrogate those curricular assumptions, this can be disconcerting. Scholarship that posits essential traits held by certain racial categories (i.e., blacks are prone to criminal activity, Asians possess a culturally superior work ethic, whites are the true progenitors of the enduring achievements of Western civilization) has not only been challenged, but cast into disrepute. Our students, as a whole, are no longer accepting the proposition that a group's basic humanity or fundamental right to be included in society is a matter open to debate. These developments are as it should be; we don't teach students that the earth is flat, that we can transform lead into gold, or that properly balancing the humors can cure a patient's illness. Why would we then leave space in higher education for similarly untrue assumptions and theorems? If we do so, we should expect pushback.

The issue is more easily grappled with in the abstract than in our institutions' complex intellectual and political climates. No, we would not invite the Grand Wizard of the Klan to speak on campus, nor would we blame our students for showing up and shouting him down if we did. But what about a speaker whose intellectual credentials rest on a book that argues that blacks are inferior to whites when it comes to intellectual capacity? If we dress a racist claim in respectable social-science discourse and have a famous white male academic write a "controversial" bestseller embracing it, does that make it something other than a racist claim? If our institution were to invite a speaker whose prominence rests on the willingness to publicly declare LGBTQIA people should not enjoy the same fundamental civil rights as heterosexuals, does the speaker's eminence and "importance" outweigh their argument that some of our students are less human than others? One might make the argument that the oft-invoked marketplace of ideas is the best way to sort the intellectual wheat from the pseudoscientific chaff, but what happens if some people have never been allowed into that marketplace to begin with? In a perfect world, sunlight would indeed be the best disinfectant. But in our imperfect world, conditioned as it is by structures of inequality and an all-pervasive history of power imbalances, it's both willfully ignorant and dangerously naive to assume that ideas rise or fall on their own merits. The claim that a marketplace of ideas will sort everything out rests on an assumption that we and our institutions live in a political, economic, and ideological vacuum. Some voices are amplified louder, some platforms are built bigger and higher, and some people get the benefit of the doubt far more often than others. And even though the world of higher education is much more diverse than it was a generation ago, those inequities remain.

In the face of actually existing inequalities and unjust hierarchies, it is unrealistic and unfair to expect our students to tacitly accept the status quo, whether it manifests itself in an exclusively Eurocentric reading list or in a campus event sponsored by an anti-LGBTQIA organization. We should not be in the business of pushing some of our students to the margins, or even out, of our community. Yet that happens on our campuses and in our classrooms far more than we know or would expect. What is the recourse for those students on the margins, especially when it appears that the institution itself is arrayed against them? What are black students supposed to do when an officially invited speaker is at the podium with the university's seal on it, delivering a speech for which he will be paid out of university funds, that implies they are intellectually inferior to others because of their race? What are undocumented students supposed to do when a speaker invited by their university, a speaker who revels in being "provocative" by identifying undocumented people by name from the podium, calls for their deportation? Where do these students get to enter the fabled marketplace of ideas? Where are their platform and microphone? Why are they expected to be decorous and courteous, when they are being told—both implicitly and explicitly—that they do not belong in this space, one to which they should have an equal claim? When we are honest and unafraid enough to think about the answers to these questions, we realize how lamentations about students' manners and calls for "civility" are no more than an effort to silence already marginalized voices. Who is calling for civility, and who is expected to be civil? *Civility is never neutral.*

Naming the Problem

Given all of this, why does so much of the campus speech discourse have an overweening emphasis on civility and decorum for marginalized students? Why is there a significant portion of conversation about pedagogical tools like safe spaces and trigger warnings that sees empathy and compassion as fatal flaws? Part of the answer to these questions is the same explanation for why impoverished people are seen as having some inherent moral failing that's made them poor, or why black Americans are told to "just get over slavery." As a society, we collectively struggle to do the hard work of naming and confronting systems of inequality. It's much easier to believe a poor person is too lazy to pull themselves up by their bootstraps than it is to acknowledge we live in historically unprecedented levels of economic inequality that make exhortations about bootstrapping nothing more than a cruel joke. It's easier for a white person to think their black colleague has a victim complex than for them to admit even though one may not be a racist themselves, they live in a racist system that consistently advantages people who look like them. It's an avoidance mechanism; acknowledging structural inequalities means we commit ourselves to either working against them or ignoring them, with all the consequences for others—acknowledged or not—that decision entails.

So it goes with higher education. It's easier to mock purportedly "triggered" students as "snowflakes" than it is to honestly reckon with the structures of inequality in which they've lived and are being asked to function. In our neoliberal frame of reference, society is organized on market principles optimized to produce individual opportunity and efficiencies.[4] Failures, deficits, struggles, or other similar features of students' stories must be the fault of those students, then; why don't they just work harder, or get more money, or choose a better school? Our prevailing cultural values tell us that success and failure are individual choices, not the mingling of individual actions with larger structures. To admit otherwise is to pull back the curtain on the neoliberal Oz. But what if we were brave enough to take down that curtain? What would we learn? What would we do differently? If we teach because we believe that it's an assertion of hope even—especially—in this bleak climate, then our teaching has to subvert this oppressive paradigm.

To teach from a place of radical hope is to refuse to accept this hostile and dehumanizing narrative about our students. It is to affirm elements of our pedagogical practice that fly in the face of dominant cultural tropes and elite disdain for the diversity and complexity of our students' experiences and needs. It is to remain committed to a vision of higher education that sees students as our allies, not our adversaries, and that supports them in efforts to take risks and overcome adversity. And it is a realization that this commitment comes from an effective praxis, a realization that our theoretical commitments have to be embodied in our everyday practice of teaching and learning with and among our students. This all holds true for the individual classroom and for institutions writ large—even when it's not fashionable or easy to embrace.

INTO PRACTICE

Think about the ways in which your teaching practices—with respect to either methods, content, or both—attempt to balance free expression and the diversity of your students. Have there been class discussions where things have gotten heated, or even gone off the rails, when students are confronted with controversial topics or others' disagreement? How have you typically handled such situations when they've arisen? In retrospect, did the techniques you used in those moments mitigate or exacerbate the power imbalances among you and your students?

Consider convening a group of students whom you know well and who are engaged in the life of your institution (a group of upper-level majors, perhaps, or the leaders of various student organizations), and conducting a focus group discussion. What are the narratives these students have been told about their education, and their place(s) within the institution? Do those narratives align with faculty and staff perceptions? How might student voices become more involved in discussions about the climate on your campus?

—

CHAPTER 10

I DON'T KNOW...YET

—

After twenty years teaching in higher education, I have concluded the three most powerful words we can say to our students might just be "I don't know." Yet in the beginning of my teaching career I was scared to death of using them. Graduate education in most of our disciplines rarely does a good job preparing us to be effective classroom teachers (if it even pays attention to pedagogy at all). Part of the reason for this, I think, is that the mindset we're encouraged to develop as master's or doctoral students runs counter to that which makes for effective teaching and learning. To admit not knowing something in a graduate seminar was tantamount to a public self-flagellation, leading us to sometimes far outkick our coverage when adding to the conversation. *Of course I've read Foucault; I mean, who couldn't see the theoretical application of his . . . uh . . . theories . . . in this case?* I know that what I perceived to be graduate school pressures, both formal and informal, led me to refuse to admit any gap, no matter how small, in my knowledge. In retrospect, this performative aspect to academic conversations wasn't something my mentors encouraged so much as it was some-thing in the air, inhaled in colloquia, seminars, conferences, and intellectual sparring at various coffee shops and pubs. I'm not sure it served me well in my PhD endeavors, and I know it served me poorly when I started teaching my own courses. It had been hard enough being a TA who was only a few years older than some of my students, but when I got an adjunct gig teaching evening courses at a local women's college, most of my students were older than I. To compen-sate for what I imagined were dubious stares and doubts about how well I, a young white dude, could teach them, a racially diverse class of older students, I resolved to be prepared for any eventuality and to dazzle them with my command of the material. What this meant, above all, was to never admit I didn't know the answer to a question, to never show any cracks in the facade of brilliance I imagined myself wrapped within. Subconsciously (though sometimes quite consciously), I was afraid that if those cracks appeared, the whole thing would come crashing down, and someone would show up to escort me out of the building since only real experts were allowed to teach students there, and just who the hell did I think I was anyway?

Clearly, graduate school did what it does so well and laid a nice case of impostor syndrome on me. Beyond that, though, I wasn't ready to deal with the disconnect between what worked (or seemed to work) for conferences and seminars and what was necessary for me to be effective in the class-room. I'm sure my case wasn't unique at all; I've had numer-ous conversations with graduate students and new faculty who point to a similar phenomenon in their own teaching. What I've learned, though, is that coming into class with my defenses up meant that I'd already lost the thing I was fight-ing for. I thought students wanted to hear from someone who knew everything about the subject, a font of knowledge from which they could draw throughout the course. What I found out was that students wanted a professor who took them seriously as learners and actual humans—and who did not take himself so seriously as to prevent that.

I was asking my students to take risks in my class. I wanted them to engage in challenging discussions of difficult material, where issues would not be easily resolved and where they would have to learn to live with ambiguity. I wanted them to stretch their intellects, to work out analytical processes collaboratively, to trust that the rest of the class would help them do so. But I wasn't doing any of that myself. I didn't trust myself or my students enough to admit I didn't know something, so I would provide answers to their questions that were either evasive or obfuscatory. College students tend to have pretty finely calibrated bullshit detectors, and I have no doubt at all the students in this course saw my know-it-all-ness for what it really was. They were reluctant to take analytical leaps, to stretch their perspective like I wanted them to, because they sensed that I wouldn't reciprocate. They were leery about admitting when they didn't know an answer or understand a concept because they saw me scramble to never go without an answer and get defensive when they asked a follow-up question. I had offloaded all of the cognitive and emotional labor onto the class and performed none of it myself. I was modeling the exact opposite of what I wanted my students to do, and unsurprisingly, they placed more weight on my actions, not my words.

I'm probably making the class sound like it went worse than it really did. If you had asked the students how the semester went, they probably would have answered "ehhh . . . fine," in much the same way that my junior high school daughter answers when I ask her "how was school today?"

"Fine" is the default answer; things went as one probably expected, no more and no less. But there wasn't anything that rose above that baseline to elicit more of a reaction than "fine, I guess" accompanied by a slight shrug. I didn't get into teaching to have things be merely "fine," though, and it was a rude awakening to finally realize that the things I claimed as central truths in my teaching philosophy were the very things I was refusing to model when I was actually with my students.

It's one thing to say we want our students to take risks, but I'm not sure we always take the time to fully unpack what that means in practice. In what is an eminently rational and understandable stance, students are reluctant to take risks if the consequences of a poor outcome outweigh the rewards of successfully meeting the challenge. It's a question of motivation—in particular, *demotivation*. What are the factors that demotivate students against the type of risk-taking and intellectual heavy lifting we want to foster in our classrooms? A significant part of the answer here lies in an understanding of how our students are themselves works in progress as we encounter them. For many of them (in particular, our first-year students), the seemingly simple act of challenging prior assumptions can be fraught with risk. For others, there is a fear they don't yet possess the necessary tools to accomplish what they think we're asking of them. Where our students perceive they are matters deeply when it comes to their academic confidence. If they see themselves as complete novices, or as learners being asked to process material they see as irrelevant, that confidence will be in short supply. Our task is to create a learning space that can help compensate for those gaps in student confidence, and encourage at least an attempt at the learning activity.

Even the most well-designed course or particular activity

avails us nothing if the climate in which we put it into operation places obstacles between our students and their learning. Outcomes are not self-actualizing. Paying careful attention to the ways in which we shape the climate of our learning spaces—physical classrooms or otherwise—should be an important part of our regular teaching practice. Moreover, as the power of the "hidden curriculum" demonstrates, it's often the choices we aren't even aware we've made that have the most impact on climate—and thus, learning. The messages our students receive from us, from one another, and from the climate in which they're trying to learn are powerful ones. How can we cultivate a learning environment that sends the message we seek to convey: that all students are welcome and can be successful, even when challenged? I would suggest that the best answer here is a counterintuitive one: in order to cultivate a space that welcomes students and promises to help them become successful learners, the climate in our classes needs to be one in which it's all right—indeed one where students are encouraged—to take risks and, most importantly, understand and admit that sometimes the result of this risk-taking can be failure.

Giving Permission to Fail

How do the promise of adversity and the threat of failure create a welcoming climate? The very proposition seems absurd on its face. Failure is a scary concept for anyone in higher education, but for students it is the quintessential representation of everything they have been conditioned to avoid. An F grade carries a stigma; there is no credit that accrues from it, as if the course in which it was "earned" never happened. An F is a dead weight on one's GPA, one that needs four or five times its mass in As to overcome. This is the way that almost all of our students have been assessed through much of their academic careers, from the middle grades forward. I can still vividly recall the miserable sinking feeling when I opened the grade report for my first semester of college and saw the F (in Intermediate Latin; *conatus malum* indeed!) staring back at me. I was told to challenge myself, so I had registered for the language course that I thought would push me. Well, I'd been pushed, all right; pushed down around a cumulative GPA of 2.0. In retrospect, I see clearly how that failing grade (and a few other close calls) was the product of a series of poor decisions on my part that made it impossible to succeed in such a demanding course. At that moment, though, all I could think was that I had *failed*.

Now that I'm on the other side of the figurative podium, I know that failure is an essential part of learning, that given the chance to reflect upon academic adversity and take appropriate action, students can learn and grow in impressive ways.[1] We're often told this, aren't we—that we should give students opportunities to fail in order that they might reap these larger benefits? To be sure, the suggestion that we create opportunities to fail is frequently accompanied by the recommendation that we do so in a low-stakes environment, one that blunts the sharp edges of that adversity. It all sounds good, but whenever I hear this type of admonition, all I can think of is how sick I felt when I saw that F in December 1990. I don't want any of my students to feel that way, even as I realize that for some of them, F grades will indeed be part of their academic experience. The question thus becomes one of preparing students to encounter that failure with the tools to render it merely an interruption in, not the end of, the story of their higher education. In order to do so, we have to carefully cultivate the spaces in which risk-taking and the encounters with failure likely to ensue can be experienced in ways that prompt both reflection and metacognitive action. This, in turn, will create a learning environment marked by mutual respect, trust, and the understanding that at its best, learning is a collective enterprise.

None of us—either we or our students—are fully formed intellects, and we should embrace the reality that learning is always and already a process of *becoming*—the quality Amy Collier and Jen Ross have aptly termed "not-yetness."[2] If we are incomplete, then there are plenty of opportunities for growth; but our initial attempts will likely fall short or perhaps miss the mark entirely. Moreover, we know from work in student development theory that our students come to us not yet the learners they will be in a week, a semester, a year, or twenty years. The classic articulation of this developmental arc is that of William G. Perry, whose influential 1968 book *Forms of Intellectual and Ethical Development in the College Years: A Scheme* laid out four stages by which we might understand a student's journey to more complex and difficult ways of thinking.[3] According to Perry, students typically begin their college years operating in a "dualistic" framework, where knowledge is fixed in nature and dispensed by authorities like professors and textbooks. Put simply, something is either right or wrong, and this dualism often evinces students' desire for us to "just tell me what's right" (or what's on the exam), as if there is one set of "correct facts" out there simply waiting to be uncovered. However, this dualism isn't sustainable; students will quickly find it an inadequate paradigm with which to explain the information they're encountering. For Perry, this sort of paradigmatic breakdown is the catalyst for moving into the next stage, and the college years are largely the story of this motion into stages two through four (multiplicity, relativism, and commitment) of their development. While Perry's original work might be seen as dated, subsequent scholarship has refined his approach by incorporating considerations like moral reasoning and gender identity into this developmental schema.[4]

Perry's theory is perhaps the most widely known, but certainly not the only, explanatory framework for student development. Arthur Chickering and Zelda Gamson, famous for their article on "Seven Principles of Good Practice in Undergraduate Education," posited a model outlining seven "vectors" that embrace such facets as intellectual, impersonal, and identity development. More recently, Rita Hardiman and Bailey Jackson described the stages of what they termed "racial identity development" for both white and African American students.[5] Their work complements a number of studies examining identity development for a variety of student populations (Asian and Asian American, Jewish, disabled, and LGBTQIA students, for example).[6] The larger insight conveyed by this literature is that we ought to be attuned to the ways in which students are developing as both learners *and* as the complex human beings they are, and how those developmental processes are unfolding in complex and uneven ways within the learning spaces where we work with and among them. In particular, Perry's insight about how a paradigm crisis is the catalyst for this developmental process seems particularly salient. It's primarily through the learner's failure to be able to explain or analyze the reality in front of them that they are forced to recognize the inadequacy of their existing framework and move into a more complex and nuanced way of being and knowing. This isn't an easy realization, to be sure; cognitive dissonance, anxiety, and defensiveness more often than not characterize this type of paradigm shift. That simply underscores the need, however, for us to cultivate spaces in which students can confront adversity, even failure, in ways that further their development rather than halt the process.

In simpler terms, then, learning is messy. The deeper and more challenging the learning tasks, the messier the process is likely to be, especially if we are asking our students to do things they have not been asked to do before. We should push our students to test their limits, we should problematize the assumptions they brought with them to college, and we should challenge them to step outside the comfortable and familiar. However, simply doing those things without a corresponding degree of scaffolding and support is more akin to hazing than it is teaching. Rigor simply for rigor's sake accomplishes little. Skillful and compassionate challenges, though, where we model the type of academic courage we're asking our students to demonstrate, can produce deep and lasting learning. To put it bluntly, we can't ask our students to take risks if we aren't willing to do the same ourselves. We can't tell our students how to learn from failure if we haven't done so ourselves. And we can't tell our students we will support them as they take risks if they don't trust we will indeed do so. What might this type of modeling look like in operation? There will, of course, be some variation across disciplines and course levels, but we can identify some common practices that allow our students to practice risk-taking and experience failure in a controlled environment. Furthermore, we can also model the practices of reflection and resilience, academic strategies that can serve our students well.

Modeling Failure

Creating a safe environment, one in which every student feels valued and supported by their peers and instructor, is the sine qua non of any class that has any aspirations of being beyond just damning-with-faint-praise "fine." The most direct and effective way for us to create that climate is to model it. Only by living our ideals can we build an authentic community with and among our students that can foster risk-taking and reflective learning. If I want my students to take risks, they ought to see me take those same kinds of risks. Only then have I modeled the type of community I exhort them to help create. *That's* why I've come to believe that the three most powerful words a teacher can say are "I don't know" (and the next three are "let's find out"). Admitting gaps in my knowledge, it turns out, didn't diminish students' respect for me as a scholar or teacher; quite the opposite, in fact. *"Great question—I'm not sure exactly where the Plague started in Europe. Let's find that out, and figure out why that geography matters"* is a discussion starter; throwing out a vague answer and silently praying it's correct is not. Simply recalling specific content isn't how we would effectively demonstrate student learning. Instead, we want them to know what to *do* with that information. We want them to be information literate, to critically assess sources, to know how to put an argument together and deploy evidence in its support. Modeling that process of retrieval—*"I don't know; let's look that up"*—is a much better pedagogical strategy than merely offering a guess or skimming past the question. It also offers us the chance to show our students where the controversies or ambiguities are in our disciplines. *"Scientists still argue about this very question." "There's a lot of disagreement over how to interpret Desdemona's character; what do you think?" "Some studies have concluded those factors are correlated, but I haven't looked at the data closely enough to know if I agree. Let's see how they did their stats."* What better way to demonstrate that scholarship isn't passing an immutable set of "facts" down through the generations, but rather a conversation where we are constantly testing, and if necessary revising, assumptions? Students are more likely to meaningfully understand that contested nature of scholarship, and thus more confidently enter those conversations, if they don't see failure as an intellectual or social death sentence. Students place a high value on endeavors we undertake with them, rather than merely command them to do themselves. And they'll acquire that essential sense of control by being agents (as opposed to mere observers) in a scholarly process where they have permission to not be perfect.

One of the most effective ways to grant that permission, which I believe can take a significant degree of unacknowledged but still powerful pressure off everyone's shoulders, is to allow students to see how we ourselves have used failure as an experience to spur growth or resilience. In my own teaching, when my students and I are working through the process of scholarly research and writing, I talk about the process by which my first journal article, written while I was still a grad student, saw publication. I show them the readers' reports from the paper's initial submission, which were . . . not great. There was little enthusiasm from any of the readers, and one in particular (Reviewer 2, naturally) had significant reservations about my article's argument and my writing style—reservations they made abundantly and bluntly clear. Then I share the email I got from the journal editor accompanying this discouraging feedback. He urged me to consider undertaking the suggested revisions, even though they were extensive and substantial, because he believed there was a publishable article somewhere in that draft, and he wanted me to try and get it out. I decided to do those revisions, which took months, and resubmit my paper. Finally, I show my students the reader reports for that revised submission: they were uniformly positive and each recommended publication. But, I reminded the students, it took a year and a half, as well as rewriting significant chunks of the paper, to get from initial submission to final acceptance. The scholarly process they were embarking on is a difficult one, I told them, but I had experience with that difficulty; I understood what it meant to experience initial failure, and as a result I could help them turn it into a growth experience.

The first time I did this activity, I was teaching a research methods course where our majors were, most for the first time, tasked with conducting extensive historical research and writing a substantial, scholarly paper. It had a reputation of being an intimidating class, and I was looking for ways to demystify the research and writing process, to demonstrate to my students that scholarly work is always in the process of becoming, that it's the product not only of our own work, but of conversation and collaboration with peers. I figured documenting my own experience would humanize things, and show them that even I, the "expert," didn't produce papers that sprang fully formed from my head, but needed the writing, rewriting, and peer review process in the same way they would as they undertook their work for the course. I promised I wouldn't review their work in the same fashion that Reviewer 2 (it's *always* Reviewer 2!) used for mine, and that the ultimate focus of any review—peer or instructor—was to make the project better. The students' feedback about this particular session was striking. Several of them commented on my course evaluations how they appreciated not only this peek behind the scholarly publishing curtain, but that I showed them how I encountered difficulties and setbacks in the same type of activity I was asking them to perform. One even thanked me for respecting them enough to share that initial failure with them. I am convinced (and subsequent feedback has affirmed) this modeling of risk-taking, sharing my experience of failure, helped my students feel more confident and willing to stretch themselves intellectually in their own research.

A caveat, however: as a tenured white male professor, I can undertake this sharing from a relatively secure position. We know that professors who are women (particularly younger faculty) and faculty of color are often not afforded the same kind of implicit respect from students (or, regrettably, some of their colleagues). Studies have shown, for example, that an African American woman is significantly more likely than I am to have her expertise doubted, perhaps even her credentials questioned, by (especially white male) students.[7] Compounding the issue, and creating a very real academic intersectionality, adjunct or sessional faculty have positions that are precarious by institutional definition. In other words, there are a number of facets to their identity that can make a faculty member vulnerable to challenges to their authority and expertise. In this case, sharing personal setbacks—at least in the early phases of a course—might exacerbate an already difficult situation and thus wouldn't be the appropriate means to accomplish the goal of community and fostering a risk-taking environment. I don't want to suggest that someone engage in what could essentially be self-sabotage for the sake of modeling risk-taking. For a faculty member who feels like they occupy a more precarious position vis-à-vis their students, it's possible, and perhaps better, to have these discussions in a less personal and more general context.

In the end, though, however we end up encouraging our students to take risks and to treat failure as a learning opportunity, it's still the work of creating the essential foundation for a truly inclusive, hopeful learning space. It's not enough to have an intellectual understanding of the necessarily incomplete nature of our learning narratives; we have to embrace our "not-yetness" and be willing to empathize with students who are themselves just coming to see their own not-yetness. All of the things we say we want a class space to be—respectful, collegial, rigorous, safe, interactive, dynamic, exciting—are products of a climate where we and our students work as collaborators rather than occupy opposite points of some academic spectrum. If we model the ways in which we want our students to venture out of their comfort zones and engage in some academic risk-taking, and create a safe environment in which they can practice doing so, then we are also fostering a class climate with all of those qualities to which we aspire. One is the function of the other. When we model constructive ways to engage with adversity and failure, we are also giving our students (and ourselves) that vital permission to be not-perfect, not-expert, not-polished . . . and not-yet. It's in the liminal spaces between not knowing and engaged understanding that deep and meaningful learning occurs. Those spaces are where old paradigms give way to new ways of knowing and understanding, a process that might—but does not have to—be fraught and risky. A learning environment that encourages students to occupy those spaces without anxiety, where structure and support are available to those who need it, is an environment in which the project of higher education functions at its best. If we want that project to shape a better future, if we want to embody hope in our pedagogical practice, then it's imperative for us to assiduously cultivate that environment and serve as its stewards.

INTO PRACTICE

Consider journaling about the time in your own academic journey where you felt failure most acutely. Was there a faculty member who played a part in this story, and if so, what was their role in the next steps you took? What lessons does this experience offer for your own interactions with students who have fallen short or encountered adversity?

What are the options your students have available to them should they fail an assignment in your course, such as an exam or essay? Is the failing grade the end of that particular story, or are there ways to promote learning from that experience of failure for your students? Consider strategies you might adopt to allow students the opportunity to learn from initial experiences of failure: perhaps revisions or rewrites accompanied by a brief self-reflection, or allowing them to submit corrections (researched and cited) for an examination for partial grade credit.

RADICAL HOPE, EVEN WHEN IT SEEMS HOPELESS

It is perhaps appropriate that the concluding chapter of this manifesto advocating for radical hope takes risk and failure for its subjects. After all, to take one's stand in an ethic of radical hope is a tenuous proposition in these times, fraught as they are with angry, resurgent, and vitriolic racism and misogyny, and in which higher education confronts an array of challenges to its very existence. It is risky to embody a pedagogy grounded in radical hope when the work that accompanies that stance can call into question some of the basic "agreements" shaping the institutional environments in which many of us are operating. And, most distressingly, sometimes hope goes unfulfilled. We might act from a place of radical hope, yet still fail to effect, or even make progress toward, the changes we seek. Indeed, depending upon the institutional and employment contexts we're in, the odds of failure might well outweigh those of success.

What then?

This is where we do for ourselves what we do for our students—cultivate an environment where failure is a setback, not a conclusion. One important way in which we might do so is to remember the "radical" part of radical hope: our approach to teaching and learning is informed by a root-level, fundamental commitment to hope. That commitment is borne out in our everyday practices, and in the learning spaces and interactions with students those practices shape. And, most essentially, those practices embody a stance grounded in a tangible praxis that consistently affirms hope over cynicism. To teach with radical hope means:

- our pedagogy embodies a lively, dynamic approach to learning, seeing both knowledge and students as always in the process of becoming,
- we treat our students as active agents in their learning, and respect and value them for the full and complicated humans that they are,
- committing to a student-centered praxis that sees learning as transformational, as opposed to merely transactional,
- we embrace inclusive pedagogy, course design, and teaching methods,
- we name the systems of inequality that shape our society and commit to blunting their power by creating learning spaces guided by the principles of equity and access,
- promoting collaboration to empower our students in cocreating the environments in which all can learn,
- even the most routine and mundane aspects of a course—such as the syllabus—are suffused with this emancipatory pedagogical vision,

- the structures we create and the practices we undertake do not marginalize any of our students; that we understand the ways in which power and authority shape teaching and learning spaces and act accordingly,
- we are vocal opponents of any institutional climate or practices that act to dehumanize anyone,
- we cultivate and sustain learning environments that are both challenging and supportive, allowing students to face risks and adversity in ways that promote persistence and growth.

These tenets cannot be put into operation without a commitment to bridge theory and practice. Our advocacy of a better future, as well as our mission of empowering our students to help create it, depends on praxis. Hope is aspirational, but also depends upon agency. For our students to see themselves as active, empowered learners—as people who can and should participate in the processes of knowledge creation and scholarly discourse—they need to work within learning spaces that cultivate that understanding. The work we should be about, then, is to create these spaces throughout whichever part of the higher educational landscape we find ourselves in.

Yet the act of creation is only the first task; maintaining and sustaining those spaces are the vital parts of a practice grounded in radical hope. Moments of pedagogical liberation that spring into existence, but evaporate just as quickly, avail us nothing; in fact, their very evanescence promotes frustration rather than fulfillment. Only through a continuing praxis, a consistent and durable commitment to putting our foundational principles into actual operation, can we effect the changes we seek and offer all of our students the opportunity to meaningfully learn and succeed. Embracing praxis, and understanding that it's carried out most effectively through the choices we make and actions we undertake on an everyday basis, helps us sustain ourselves even in times that seem to militate against hope. Change in higher education can sometimes occur dramatically; perhaps an institution revises its mission, or alters its admissions policy, or—on the negative side—closes down. But these episodes of dramatic change are rare, and not always durable. The real work of change in higher education is done student by student, classroom by classroom, course by course, and it's done by educators who have committed to teaching because it and their students *matter*. In working for this change, we not only invigorate our own practices, we commit to helping build a vibrant and critical culture of teaching and learning in our institutions. And perhaps most important of all, we do better by and for our students. Doing what we do, being intentional about doing it well, and defending its worth boldly and intelligently are defiant assertions that things can and will get better. Tens of thousands of teachers in higher education are doing those things every day—compelling evidence to the power of teaching as a radical act of hope.

NOTES

INTRODUCTION

1. "Sharp Partisan Divisions in Views of National Institutions," Pew Research Center, July 10, 2017, http://www.people-press .org/2017/07/10/sharp-partisan-divisions-in-views-of-national -institutions.
2. "Completing College—National—2018," National Student Clearinghouse Research Center, December 18, 2018, https:// nscresearchcenter.org/signaturereport16.
3. "Campus Sexual Violence: Statistics," RAINN, https://www .rainn.org/statistics/campus-sexual-violence.
4. See, for example, Jeremy Bauer-Wolf, "Hate Incidents on Campus Still Rising," *Inside Higher Ed*, February 25, 2019, https://www.insidehighered.com/news/2019/02/25/hate -incidents-still-rise-college-campuses.
5. Jonathan Lear, *Radical Hope: Ethics in the Face of Cultural Devastation* (Cambridge, MA: Harvard University Press, 2008), loc. 1029, Kindle.
6. Lear, *Radical Hope*, loc. 1046, Kindle.
7. Rebecca Solnit, *Hope in the Dark: Untold Histories, Wild Possibilities*, 3rd ed. (Chicago: Haymarket Books, 2016), 4.
8. Paulo Freire, *Pedagogy of the Oppressed*, 30th anniversary ed. (New York: Continuum, 2000), 126 (emphasis in original).

CHAPTER 1

1. N. F. S. Grundtvig, "The School for Life and the Academy in Sorø (1838)," in *The School for Life: N. F. S. Grundtvig on Education for the People*, trans. Edward Broadbridge, eds. Clay Warren and Uffe Jonas (Aarhus, Denmark: Aarhus University Press, 2011), 187–208.

2. Tomasz Maliszewski, ed., *School for Life: Guide to the Contemporary Folk High Schools* (Grzybów, Poland: Ecological and Cultural Association ZIARNO, 2016).

3. bell hooks, *Teaching to Transgress: Education as the Practice of Freedom* (New York: Routledge, 1994); Paulo Freire, *Education for Critical Consciousness* (New York: Continuum, 1973).

4. The call for using these two "languages" runs throughout much of Giroux's work. See, for example, Henry A. Giroux, *Pedagogy and the Politics of Hope: Theory, Culture, and Schooling* (Boulder, CO: Westview Press, 1997), esp. part 2.

5. Nick Roll, "When Your Students Attend White Supremacist Rallies," *Inside Higher Ed*, Aug. 15, 2017, https://www.insidehighered.com/news/2017/08/15/college-students-unmasked-unite-right-protesters; Greg Toppo, "Education for All . . . Even a 'Nazi'?" *Inside Higher Ed*, Sept. 27, 2018, https://www.insidehighered.com/news/2018/09/27/university-tests-free-speech-mettle-ensuring-graduation-charlottesville-marcher.

6. Horace Mann, "Report for 1848: The Capacity of the Common-School System to Improve the Pecuniary Condition, and Elevate the Intellectual, Moral, and Religious Character, of the Commonwealth" in *Life and Works of Horace Mann*, Vol. 3, ed. Mary Mann (Boston: Horace B. Fuller, 1868), 669.

7. See the discussion of this strain of argument in Jennifer Simpson, *Longing for Justice: Higher Education and Democracy's Agenda* (Toronto: University of Toronto Press, 2014), 48–55 (quoted at 49).

8. On the racist appropriations of the Middle Ages, see *The Public Medievalist*'s series "Race, Racism, and the Middle Ages," https://www.publicmedievalist.com/race-racism-middle-ages-toc; also see the statement by *Medievalists of Color*, "On Race and Medieval Studies," http://medievalistsofcolor.com/statements/on-race-and-medieval-studies/.

9. Henry Giroux, "Charlottesville, Neo-Nazis, and the Challenge to Higher Education" [orig. 2017], in Jennifer A. Sandlin and Jake Burdick, eds., *The New Henry Giroux Reader* (Gorham, ME: Myers Education Press, 2019), 371–75 (quoted at 373).

10. Paulo Freire, *Pedagogy of Hope: Reliving Pedagogy of the Oppressed* (London: Bloomsbury, 2014), loc. 2630, Kindle.

11. Laura Rendón, *Sentipensante (Sensing/Thinking) Pedagogy: Educating for Wholeness, Social Justice, and Liberation* (Sterling, VA: Stylus, 2009), 24–27.

12. Henry A. Giroux, "Utopian Thinking in Dangerous Times: Critical Pedagogy and the Project of Educated Hope," in *Utopian*

Pedagogy: Radical Experiments against Neoliberal Globalization, ed. Mark Coté, Richard J. F. Day, and Greig de Peuter (Toronto: University of Toronto Press, 2007), 25–42, quoted at 37 (emphasis added).

13. Paulo Freire, *Pedagogy of the Oppressed,* 30th anniversary ed. (New York: Continuum, 2000), 71.

14. Amy Collier and Jen Ross, "For Whom, and for What? Not-yetness and Thinking Beyond Open Content," *Open Praxis* 9, no. 1 (2017), http://dx.doi.org/10.5944/openpraxis.9.1.406. Collier and Ross use this concept in their discussion of learning and technology in the context of open online learning, but their emphasis on "risk, uncertainty, and messiness" as essential components of the learning process (a response to dominant pedagogies that embody "a rhetoric of control, efficiency, and enhancement") is a valuable pedagogical insight whatever the educational context.

15. Freire, *Pedagogy of the Oppressed,* n87.

CHAPTER 3

1. Laura I. Rendón, *Sentipensante (Sensing/Thinking) Pedagogy: Educating for Wholeness, Social Justice, and Liberation* (Sterling, VA: Stylus Publishing, 2009), 25–48.

2. David Foster Wallace, "This is Water," (commencement speech, Kenyon College, Gambier, OH, May, 21, 2005), http://bulletin-archive.kenyon.edu/x4280.html.

3. See, for example, Martin A. Conway, Gillian Cohen, and Nicola Stanhope, "On the Very Long-Term Retention of Knowledge Acquired through Formal Education: Twelve Years of Cognitive Psychology," *Journal of Experimental Psychology: General* 120 (1991): 395–409. For the difference evident in students who regularly revisit and apply material in new contexts versus those who do not, see Andrew Pawl, Analia Barrantes, David E. Pritchard, and Rudolph Mitchell, "What Do Seniors Remember from Freshman Physics?" *Physical Review Special Topics—Physics Education Research* 8 (2012): 020118-1–020118-12. Two excellent overviews of the ways in which memory, cognition, and learning are intertwined are Daniel Willingham, *Why Don't Students Like School? A Cognitive Scientist Answers Questions about How the Mind Works and What It Means for the Classroom* (San Francisco: Jossey-Bass, 2010) and Peter C. Brown, Henry L. Roediger III, and Mark A. McDaniel, *Make It Stick: The Science of Successful Learning* (Cambridge, MA: Harvard University Press, 2014).

4.   Quoted in Ana Maria Araujo Freire and Donaldo Macedo, eds., *The Paulo Freire Reader* (New York: Continuum, 1998), 69.
5.   Freire and Macedo, *Freire Reader*, 70–71.
6.   Freire and Macedo, *Freire Reader*, 71.
7.   bell hooks, *Teaching to Transgress: Education as the Practice of Freedom* (New York: Routledge, 1994).
8.   Paulo Freire, *Pedagogy of the Oppressed*, 30th anniversary ed. (New York: Continuum, 2000), 126.
9.   Maryellen Weimer, *Learner-Centered Teaching: Five Key Changes to Practice* (San Francisco: Jossey-Bass, 2002), xii.

CHAPTER 4

1.   Megan Kate Nelson, "I'm a Social Media Sexist (and, Probably, You Are Too)," *Historista*, http://www.megankatenelson.com/im-a-social-media-sexist-and-probably-you-are-too. Subsequently, the #WomenAlsoKnowHistory Twitter hashtag continues to highlight the ways in which gender shapes scholarly discourse and its amplification within my home discipline.
2.   This is a point powerfully made by Cia Verschelden in her book *Bandwidth Recovery: Helping Students Reclaim Cognitive Resources Lost to Poverty, Racism, and Social Marginalization* (Sterling, VA: Stylus, 2017). See esp. pp. 5–30.
3.   Frank Tuitt, "Inclusive Pedagogy: Implications for Race, Equity, and Higher Education in a Global Context," in *Race, Equity, and the Learning Environment*, ed. Frank Tuitt, Chayla Hayes, and Saran Stewart (Sterling, VA: Stylus, 2016), 205–21, quoted at 210.
4.   On this point, see Sarah Rose Cavanagh's discussion of students' "appraisals" of value (informed by Reinhard Pekrun's control-value theory) in *The Spark of Learning: Energizing the College Classroom with the Science of Emotion* (Morgantown: West Virginia University Press, 2016), 148–57.
5.   The foundational research on stereotype threat is in Claude M. Steele and Joshua Aronson, "Stereotype Threat and the Intellectual Test Performance of African Americans," *Journal of Personality and Social Psychology* 69, no. 5 (Nov. 1995), 797–811. Steele synthesizes much of the work on stereotype threat in his *Whistling Vivaldi: How Stereotypes Affect Us and What We Can Do* (New York: W. W. Norton, 2011). For the STEM context, see Marie Kendall Brown, et al., "Teaching for Retention in Science, Engineering, and Math Disciplines: A Guide for Faculty," *CRLT*

Occasional Papers, no. 25, University of Michigan Center for Research on Learning and Teaching, 2009, esp. 3–4.

6. Herbert Marcuse, "Repressive Tolerance," in *A Critique of Pure Tolerance*, ed. Robert Paul Wolff, Barrington Moore Jr., and Herbert Marcuse (Boston: Beacon Press, 1969), 95–137.

7. Stephen D. Brookfield and Stephen Preskill, *Discussion as a Way of Teaching: Tools and Techniques for Democratic Classrooms*, 2nd ed. (San Francisco: Jossey-Bass, 2005), 255.

8. Sara Ahmed, *On Being Included: Racism and Diversity in Institutional Life* (Durham, NC: Duke University Press, 2012). See also the discussion in Rendón, *Sentipensante*, 41–44.

9. The best synthesis of the research on emotion's role in cognition and learning is Cavanagh, *Spark of Learning*.

10. For an overview of this research, see Amy Lee, et al., *Teaching Interculturally: A Framework for Integrating Disciplinary Knowledge and Intercultural Development* (Sterling, VA: Stylus, 2017); Margery B. Ginsberg and Raymond J. Wlodkowski, *Diversity and Motivation: Culturally Responsive Teaching in College* (San Francisco: Jossey-Bass, 2009); and Tuitt, Haynes, and Stewart, eds., *Race, Equity, and the Learning Environment.* Refer also to the resources on "The Research Basis for Inclusive Teaching" aggregated by the University of Michigan's Center for Research on Learning and Teaching at http://www.crlt.umich .edu/research-basis-inclusive-teaching.

11. Stephen Brookfield, *Becoming a Critically Reflective Teacher* (San Francisco: Jossey-Bass, 1995), 28.

CHAPTER 5

1. "What is Universal Design for Learning?" National Center on Universal Design for Learning, http://www.udlcenter.org /aboutudl/whatisudl.

2. "UDL Guidelines," National Center on Universal Design for Learning, http://www.udlcenter.org/aboutudl/udlguidelines _theorypractice; Thomas Tobin and Kirsten Behling, *Reach Everyone, Teach Everyone: Universal Design for Learning in Higher Education* (Morgantown: West Virginia University Press, 2018).

3. See James M. Lang, "A Welcoming Classroom," *The Chronicle of Higher Education*, Sep. 27, 2017, https://www.chronicle.com /article/A-Welcoming-Classroom/241294.

4. For an overview of the benefits of diversity and inclusion across campuses and curricula, see Patricia Gurin, Eric L. Dey, Sylvia Hurtado, and Gerald Gurin, "Diversity and Higher Education:

Theory and Impact on Educational Outcomes," *Harvard Educational Review* 72, no. 3 (2002): 330–66.

5. Paulo Freire, *Pedagogy of Hope: Reliving Pedagogy of the Oppressed* (London: Bloomsbury, 2014), loc. 85–87, Kindle.

6. Henry Giroux, "On Critical Pedagogy," in *Critical Pedagogy Today*, ed. Shirley Steinberg and Ana Maria Araujo Freire (New York: Bloomsbury, 2011), chap. 1.

CHAPTER 6

1. In particular, Reinhard Pekrun's control-value theory offers us much to consider about students' perceptions of control and autonomy, and how those affect motivation and cognition. See Pekrun, et al., "The Control-Value Theory of Achievement Emotions: An Integrative Approach to Emotions in Education," in *Emotions in Education*, ed. Paul A. Schutz and Reinhard Pekrun (Amsterdam: Academic Press, 1996), 13–36, and Sarah Rose Cavanagh, *The Spark of Learning: Energizing the College Classroom with the Science of Emotion* (Morgantown: West Virginia University Press, 2016), 145–63.

2. Amy Getty, "Choose Your Own Adventure: The Quest for Student Agency in an American Literature Class," *Currents in Teaching and Learning* 10, no. 1 (May 2018): 32–38.

3. Linda B. Nilson, *Specifications Grading: Restoring Rigor, Motivating Students, and Saving Faculty Time* (Sterling, VA: Stylus Publishing, 2014). For an overview of various grading systems along these lines, see Nilson's article, "Yes, Virginia, There's a Better Way to Grade," *Inside Higher Ed*, Jan. 19, 2016. https://www.insidehighered.com/views/2016/01/19 /new-ways-grade-more-effectively-essay.

4. Ryan Cordrell, "Unessays," Technologies of Texts course website, Fall 2014, http://f14tot.ryancordell.org/assignments /unessays/. See also Daniel Paul O'Donnell, "The Unessay," Sept. 4, 2012, http://people.uleth.ca/~daniel.odonnell/Teaching/the -unessay.

5. Christopher Jones, "Assigning the Unessay in the U.S. Survey," *The Junto: A Group Blog on Early American History*, June 26, 2018, https://earlyamericanists.com/2018/06/26/assigning -the-unessay-in-the-u-s-survey/.

6. Some research suggests that assignment choice correlates positively with student learning, as well as the value students assign to courses using this practice. See, for example, Catherine F. Brooks and Stacy L. Young, "Are Choice-Making Opportunities Needed in the Classroom? Using Self-Determination Theory

to Consider Student Motivation and Learner Empowerment," *International Journal of Teaching and Learning in Higher Education* 23, no. 1 (2011): 48–59 (interestingly, this study also posits that attendance policies can significantly affect students' perceptions of how valuable the learning experience is). Scholarship on blended and digital learning also finds value in assignment choice for students. A representative example is Thomas Wanner and Edward Palmer, "Personalising Learning: Exploring Student and Teacher Perceptions about Flexible Learning and Assessment in a Flipped University Course," *Computers & Education* 88 (2015): 354–69.

7. This is Paulo Freire's formulation, describing what he meant by "education as achieving critical consciousness."

CHAPTER 7

1. Ken Bain, *What the Best College Teachers Do* (Cambridge, MA: Harvard University Press, 2004), quoted in James M. Lang, "The Promising Syllabus," *Chronicle of Higher Education*, Aug. 26, 2006, https://www.chronicle.com/article/The-Promising -Syllabus/46748.

2. Mark Sample, "Accessibility Statements on Syllabuses," *ProfHacker*, Sept. 9, 2013, https://www.chronicle.com/blogs /profhacker/accessibility-statements-on-syllabuses/52079.

3. James M. Lang, *Small Teaching: Everyday Lessons from the Science of Learning* (San Francisco: Jossey-Bass, 2016), 5.

4. "Freewill," track 2 on Rush, *Permanent Waves*, Mercury Records, 1980.

CHAPTER 8

1. Mark Bauerlein, *The Dumbest Generation: How the Digital Age Stupefies Young Americans and Jeopardizes Our Future (Or, Don't Trust Anyone Under 30)* (New York: Penguin/Random House, 2009); William Deresiewicz, *Excellent Sheep: The Miseducation of the American Elite and the Way to a Meaningful Life* (New York: Free Press, 2014).

2. "University of Chicago Tells Freshmen It Does Not Support 'Trigger Warnings'," National Public Radio's *All Things Considered*, Aug. 26, 2016, https://www.npr.org/2016/08/26/491531869 /university-of-chicago-tells-freshmen-it-does-not-support -trigger-warnings.

3. John Palfrey, *Safe Spaces, Brave Spaces: Diversity and Free Expression in Education* (Cambridge, MA: MIT Press, 2017).

4. See, for example, the active forum "New Game! DEAR

STUDENT(S)," on the *Chronicle of Higher Education* website: https://www.chronicle.com/forums/index.php?topic=187597.0.
5.   Henry Giroux, "Dangerous Pedagogy in the Age of Casino Capitalism," in *America's Education Deficit and the War on Youth* (New York: Monthly Review Press), 183–215 (quoted at 199–200).

CHAPTER 9

1.   On Murray and Middlebury, see "Shouting Down a Lecture," *Inside Higher Ed*, March 3, 2017, https://www.insidehighered .com/news/2017/03/03/middlebury-students-shout-down -lecture-charles-murray; on the incidents at Berkeley, see "Milo Yiannopoulos Finally Spoke at Berkeley. But the Protesters Were Louder," *Time*, September 25, 2017, https://time .com/4955245/milo-yiannopoulos-berkeley-free-speech-week.
2.   A recent example is Jonathan Haidt and Greg Lukianoff, *The Coddling of the American Mind: How Good Intentions and Bad Ideas Are Setting a Generation Up for Failure* (New York: Penguin, 2018). But also see John Warner's insightful review on *Inside Higher Ed*, September 18, 2018, https://www.insidehighered .com/blogs/just-visiting/million-thoughts-coddling-american -mind.
3.   On race and gender, see the essential overviews in Robert Wald Sussman, *The Myth of Race: The Troubling Persistence of an Unscientific Idea* (Cambridge, MA: Harvard University Press, 2016) and Angela Saini, *Inferior: How Science Got Women Wrong, and the New Research That's Rewriting the Story* (Boston: Beacon Press, 2018).
4.   David Harvey, *A Brief History of Neoliberalism* (New York: Oxford University Press, 2005), esp. 5–38; Lawrence Busch, *Knowledge for Sale: The Neoliberal Takeover of Higher Education* (Cambridge, MA: MIT Press, 2017); Henry A. Giroux, *Neoliberalism's War on Higher Education* (Chicago: Haymarket Books, 2014).

CHAPTER 10

1.   See the excellent discussion on learning through failure in Joshua R. Eyler, *How Humans Learn: The Science and Stories behind Effective College Teaching* (Morgantown: West Virginia University Press, 2018), 171–217.
2.   In Collier's words, "Not-yetness is not satisfying every condition, **not** fully understanding something, **not** check- listing everything, **not** tidying everything, **not** trying to solve

every problem . . . but creating space for emergence to take us to new and unpredictable places, to help us better understand the problems we are trying to solve" (emphasis in original). See Amy Collier, "Not-Yetness," *The Red Pincushion*, April 9, 2015, http://redpincushion.us/blog/teaching-and-learning/not-yetness. See also Amy Collier and Jen Ross, "For Whom, and for What? Not-yetness and Thinking beyond Open Content," *Open Praxis* 9, no. 1 (2017), https://openpraxis.org/index.php/OpenPraxis/article/view/406.

3. William G. Perry, *Forms of Intellectual and Ethical Development in the College Years: A Scheme*, rev. ed. (New York: Wiley, 1998).

4. See, for example, Thomas Lickona, ed., *Moral Development and Behavior: Theory, Research, and Social Issues* (New York: Holt, Rinehart, and Winston, 1976); Marcia B. Baxter-Magolda, *Knowing and Reasoning in College: Gender-Related Patterns in Students' Intellectual Development* (San Francisco: Jossey-Bass, 1992).

5. Rita Hardiman and Bailey W. Jackson, "Racial Identity Development: Understanding Racial Dynamics in College Classrooms and on Campus," *New Directions for Teaching and Learning* 52 (1992): 21–37.

6. See the discussion of these various approaches to student development in Susan Ambrose, et al., *How Learning Works: Seven Research-Based Principles for Smart Teaching* (San Francisco: Jossey-Bass, 2010), 158–70.

7. Jeanette Morehouse Mendez and Jesse Perez Mendez, "What's in a Name . . . or a Face? Student Perceptions of Faculty Race," *Journal of Political Science Education* 14, no. 2 (2018), 177–96; Frank Tuitt, Michele Hanna, Lisa M. Martinez, María del Carmen Salazar, and Rachel Griffin, "Teaching in the Line of Fire: Faculty of Color in the Academy," *Thought and Action* 66 (2009), 65–74.

INDEX